H◆I◆N◆D◆U
E◆T◆H◆I◆C◆S

McGill Studies in the History of Religions:
A Series Devoted to International Scholarship
Katherine K. Young, Editor

HINDU ETHICS

Purity, Abortion, and Euthanasia

Harold G. Coward
Julius J. Lipner
Katherine K. Young

State University of New York Press

Published by
State University of New York Press, Albany

Printed in the United States of America

For information, address State University of New York
Press, State University Plaza, Albany, N.Y., 12246

Library of Congress Cataloging-in-Publication Data

Coward, Harold G.
Hindu ethics.

(McGill studies in the history of religions)
Includes index.
1. Hindu ethics. 2. Body, Human—Religious
aspects—Hinduism. 3. Abortion—Religious aspects—
Hinduism. 4. Euthanasia—Religious aspects—
Hinduism. I. Lipner, Julius. II. Young, Katherine K.,
1944- . III. Title. IV. Series.
BJ122.C7 1988 294.5′48697 87-18075
ISBN 0-88706-763-8
ISBN 0-88706-764-6 (pbk.)

10 9 8 7 6 5 4 3 2 1

Contents

Introduction

HAROLD G. COWARD

MODERN WESTERN approaches to India, and in particular to Hinduism, have focused on metaphysics at the expense of ethics. As a result, Westerners have often tended to see Hinduism as concerned with the esoteric, the otherwordly, the mystical, and thus as having a blind eye when it comes to the ethical issues of daily life. Western religions like Judaism and Christianity were thought to offer something lacking in Hinduism, namely, the moral vitality of the Hebrew prophets and the New Testament. It was this moral vitality that many Christian missionaries saw themselves as bringing to India to challenge an ethically lax Hinduism. *Satī* or widow burning and the making of caste distinctions were typical of the so-called heathen practices singled out by the missionaries for attack.[1]

Is Hinduism a religion which is weak or lacking in ethics? The authors of this book examine this question by analyzing Hindu teaching on three problems of significance for the modern world: purity, abortion, and euthanasia. This approach enables the reader to see what Hinduism has to say about ethical problems which are posing a serious challenge to modern scholars. In this way, the strengths and weaknesses of Hindu ethics will be immediately apparent to the Western Christian, Jew, humanist, or secularist who wrestles with how abortion, euthanasia, and purity are to be dealt with in our modern world. In this sense, these essays have importance for today's study of medical ethics, social ethics, and human rights, in that they provide a systematic analysis of these problems from the perspective of a quite different Eastern world view.

For the student of Eastern religions, these chapters are important for their exploration in depth of the ethical foundations present within Hinduism—foundations which some would say are more basic than the metaphysics of Śaṅkara and Ramanuja about which so much has been written in English. Recent scholarship has begun to draw attention to the fundamental position of ethics in Hindu thought. In his *Structural Depths of Indian Thought,*[2] P. T. Raju charts a new approach for Western graduate students studying Hinduism. Raju begins with ethics (Mīmāṃsā and the *Dharmaśāstras*) and moves from that basis to a consideration of metaphysics, such as the ontology of Śaṅkara's Vedānta. Raju justifies this approach by noting that past presentations of Indian Philosophy in English (e.g., S. Radhakrishnan's two-volume *indian philosophy*) have subsumed and equated ethics with the theories of salvation offered by the various schools. "But," says Raju, "such an equation gives rise, and has given rise to the impression that Indian thought has no idea of moral and ethical law."[3] Raju makes clear the importance of the distinction for which he is arguing:

> It is not justifiable to equate ethics and the theory of salvation . . . From the ultimate point of view, where there is no "Ought" there is no ethics. Disciplines for salvation consist of different forms of worship, breath-control, etc. Nobody is morally obliged to practice them. Most of the Indian philosophers do not regard such practices as an "Ought" (*vidhi*). But moral law is an "Ought" and the Vedantins and even the Mīmāṃsakas knew the distinction between values which are only recommended to be good. Obtaining salvation, like obtaining wealth, is not an "Ought." It is, therefore, not justifiable to equate ethics and the theory of salvation.[4]

The 'ought' of ethics (*dharma*) is foundational for all Indian thought in that it includes: the ideals for human life in this world, ones relation to other human beings, the duties of caste (*varṇa*) and the stages of life (*aśramas*). Śaṅkara suggests that his teaching of knowledge (*jñāna*) is intended to follow immediately on study of the Vedas (*pūrva mīmāṃsā,* the enquiry into *dharma*),[5] and Patañjali effectively makes the same requirement in his listing of the bad habits to be broken (*yamas*) and good habits to be established (*niyamas*) as requirements for the practise of yoga.[6] For Jaimini, ethical action (*dharma*) is inesçapable and is therefore the supreme governing force of the universe.[7]

The following chapters on purity, abortion, and euthanasia offer case study explorations into specific topics of *dharma* or Hindu Ethics—case studies which are selected and presented so as to invite comparisons with modern Western thought to develop in the critical reflection of the reader. Such comparisons, which are merely suggested here, will help to remove the apparent otherwordly nature of Hindu thought from the minds of Western readers, as well as give depth and new significance to Indian ideas on these timely topics.

In Chapter 1, Harold Coward surveys attitudes towards purity and bodily function found in the Harappā culture, the Vedas, Epics, and *Laws of Manu* but focuses on the way in which these early ideas are systematized in Patañjali's *Yoga Sūtras*. In the *Yoga Sūtras*, the three *guṇas* or qualities of *tamas* (dullness), *rajas* (passion, movement), and *sattva* (transparency) are described as having increasing qualities of purity. The yoga technique outlined by Patañjali is designed to purify the *tamas* and *rajas* from one's material nature (*prakṛti*) until one becomes virtually pure *sattva*. The *yoga sūtras*, like the Vedas and the *Laws of Manu*, see bodily discharges as polluting in nature (*tamasic*), and thus the purified yogi shrinks from contact with such substances. Since women have more bodily discharges than men, they are seen as being more impure. Menstrual blood is considered to be especially polluting, although there is ambiguity here since some classical texts treat menstrual blood as the female seed which joins with the male semen to produce the child. Some Tantric practices take the approach of using female discharges, such as menstrual blood, as a ritual drink—the idea being to use the most powerful female pollution as a means to overcome all pollution. On the whole, however, Hindus see bodily fluids as polluting and menstrual blood as especially so.

Further exemplification of Patañjali's position is found in the disciplines followed by Gorakhnāth and his followers, the Kānphaṭa Yogis, during the medieval period. Coward shows how all of this provides a basis for the logical development of a strong negative attitude toward women and persons who do not make an effort to practice cleanliness who are thus empirically seen to be of a lower quality (lower caste).

The traditional Hindu approach to purity is found to exemplify the kind of ethical and philosophical issue that the modern experience of a pluralism of world views raises. What happens when the modern Western presupposition of the right to equality comes into conflict with a traditional world view in which equality at the highest level is not a legal right but a hard won achievement resulting from good ethical choices—the doing of one's *dharma*—in this and previous lives? Such a clash occurs when Hindus who have become Canadian or American citizens, and are thus under the equality prescribed by the Charter of Rights of those countries, attempt to practice their traditional religious approach to purity and pollution, a religious practice which that same Charter of Rights guarantees. Coward examines how this conflict with the received egalitarian world view of modernity is present in the new Constitution of India. The clash between the classical Hindu view of purity and the negative attitude it establishes toward women and the lower castes is examined against the background of the equality prescribed by the Constitution of India.

In Chapter 2, Julius Lipner examines the Hindu attitude to abortion. In the classical Hindu view, the living embryo enjoys a special moral status in the eyes of the Hindu and is specially deserving of protection and respect. In the law books, the killing of a pregnant woman is given the same status as the killing of a Brahmin. Therefore, for the Hindu, pregnancy is a very special state in which the unborn have a moral status which merits special protection. It is no surprise that many Hindu texts specifically condemn abortion. Special exemplification is provided from the *Mahābhārata*. Lipner makes clear that, in spite of some suggestions in the law books that it is social status rather than morality which is at issue in cases of abortion, there is a strong moral element in the Hindu condemnation of abortion.

Lipner notes that, in the classical Hindu view, only when the mother's life is in danger in childbirth (due to a badly placed foetus) is abortion allowed. Lipner analyzes reasons why Hindus accorded the unborn such a high status. Reasons used by modern moralists (such as, the foetus has not yet attained human form or demonstrated cerebral activity) to distinguish between human persons (not acceptable to abort) and human beings (acceptable to abort) are not found or supported in classical Hindu thought. In fact, the classical Hindu view was that the soul (*jiva*) descends into the union of semen and menstrual blood in the womb and so coincides with conception. Thus no qualitative distinction can be made between conception and a later time at which the embryo is postulated to become a person. Traditional Hindu medical texts emphasize that the *jiva*, the individual abode of consciousness, is present from the moment of conception onwards through the process of foetal growth. These texts note no significant break or leap forward in this growth which would lead one to conclude that some qualitative change had taken place equivalent to the distinction suggested by some modern ethicists from human being to human person. The texts Lipner cites to prove the awareness of the foetus in the womb also reflect the impurity of the womb referred to in Coward's discussion of purity.

Abortion was also unacceptable to the classical Hindu because it interferes with the natural and necessary cycle of *karma* and rebirth. Abortion is seen as a grave infringement on the working out of an individual's destiny—especially since only during one's life could an individual make decisions which would result in the goal of enlightenment or release (*mokṣa*). By virtue of abortion, a person's chance for the realization of *mokṣa* in this life is being removed—the person's freedom is being taken away. Other reasons militating against abortion in the Hindu view are the stress on the egg or embryo as the scriptural symbol for life, the felt need to continue one's line through male heirs, the obtaining of security after death through the *śrāddha* rites performed by the heir, and finally the high status given to *ahiṃsā* or non-injury in Indian society.

In her study of the traditional Hindu view of euthanasia in Chapter 3, Katherine Young observes that, if we were to take today's emergent definition of euthanasia with its technical insistence on medically defined cases of terminal illness and its circumscribed meaning of a doctor actively killing a patient on compassionate grounds, given due process of decision making, then, by definition, we would be hard pressed to find equivalent situations in the past and in other premodern societies. To facilitate an historical and comparative study, she uses the archaic meaning of euthanasia as "freedom to leave," which permitted the sick and despondent to terminate their lives. Her study illumines how self-willed death in certain situations of old age and disease was found in India throughout much of history until it was eliminated in the early modern period. In comparison, euthanasia, in the sense of freedom to leave, was rarely found in the West after the Graeco-Roman period, although today its merits are increasingly debated, as withdrawal of treatment becomes a common phenomenon in hospitals and the debate over compassionate murder continues.

Katherine Young's analysis of the Indian sources focuses on the various forms of self-willed death: suicide; heroic, voluntary death; and religious, self-willed death. Suicide, prohibited by the traditional Hindu law books, was self-willed death prompted by passion, depression, or uncontrollable circumstance. Heroic, voluntary death was of three kinds: heroic, self-imposed death by a warrior as a way to avoid calamity, as a substitute for death in battle (which was thought to result in the attainment of heaven), and as a way to allow peaceful succession to the throne. Closely related to heroic death was religious, self-willed death, which was explicitly viewed as a means to maintain *dharma*, attain heaven, or achieve liberation; it attracted people beyond the warrior milieu and, over time, became a popular religious practice. In the Hindu context, euthanasia belonged to the category of religious self-willed death. Accordingly, it was never understood as the mercy killing of one person by another. In Hinduism, therefore, the willpower of the individual to bring about his or her own death was normative for the acceptance of euthanasia.

This Hindu perspective is shown by Young to have evolved dynamically out of the historical interaction of Hinduism with Jainism and Buddhism. In her discussion of self-willed death with reference to euthanasia, Young finds the 8th–6th century B.C.E. a significant period. She argues that the extreme violence, which accompanied the rise of kingdoms, characterized the epoch; to understand why the Vedic ideal of a life of one hundred years ending in natural death was gradually displaced, it is necessary to postulate that the various forms of heroic and religious self-willed death were alternatives to death in battle by which one attained heaven or were ways to escape violence within society.

Not only does Young develop a new theory of the origins of nonviolence in this analysis, she demonstrates how the religions came to terms with the new phenomenon of self-willed death. Jainism was likely the first religion to accept the practice of a religiously motivated, self-willed death; it was called *sallekhanā* and involved a fast to death. While Buddha tried to avoid acceptance of the heroic, self-willed death so common in Kṣatriya circles, he did allow self-willed death for the extremely ill person as an act of compassion; that is, he endorsed euthanasia. In Hinduism, Brahmanical willingness to ritualize the withdrawal by the king (and his wife) into the forest as a way of abdicating the throne in old age way may have set the stage for religious self-sacrifice and self-willed death as a way to attain heaven.

From the 6th century B.C.E. to the 10th century C.E., Young compares the Hindu law books (*Dharmaśāstras*) with Buddhist and Jain texts from the same period and finds that, while suicide is thoroughly condemned, heroic death in battle, self-imposed death by one who is enlightened or desires enlightenment, and self-willed death in extreme old age and ill health is increasingly accepted. For example, dignity in old age is safeguarded for the Hindu. When one can no longer perform daily *dharmic* duties for oneself, such as bodily purification, euthanasia is then allowed by means such as jumping from a cliff into water or jumping into fire or walking until death occurs. Religious, self-willed death also comes to be accepted in many medieval Buddhist texts, although the method differs, with cutting the throat by the sword being preferred. Here, the sword seems to symbolize the cutting out of desire and ignorance so as to usher in enlightenment.

With legitimation of self-willed death and its promise of heaven or liberation, the religions started to compete in their prescription of an easy means to achieve enlightenment. Hindu texts, for instance, promoted self-willed death at a sacred place, which was understood as a spot to cross over from this world to the next. In Mahāyāna Buddhism, the *bodhisattva* ideal of self-sacrifice, including sacrifice of one's body to help another unfortunate being, led to further popularity of the practice. Jainism, too, embraced the increasing popularity of self-willed death by extending the practice of *sallekhanā* from monastics to the laity, particularly in cases of old age and severe disease.

Young's analysis shows, however, that from the tenth century on there was increasing criticism of religious, self-willed death. Such criticism, already prevalent in Hindu circles, was greatly accentuated by the outcry of the Christian missionaries in the 18th and 19th centuries. Young includes in this discussion a very helpful analysis of *satī* or the burning of a widow on her husband's funeral pyre. Young also notes that modern Jains continue to practice *sallekhanā*, the fast to death, and carefully distinguish it from non-religious suicide which is prohibited by the Indian Penal Code. The modern reassessment of euthanasia in India has been led, in fact, by the Jains who argue that in Jainism *sallekhanā* was not abused; on the contrary, it provided a meaningful and dignified death that was in tune with the religious perspective.

Young concludes from her study of euthanasia in Hinduism and, by extension, in other Indian religions that it was extremely difficult to limit euthanasia to certain contexts and to prevent abuse even when there was a strong religious predisposition to live out the natural life span. She suggests that there are two basic approaches regarding the reassessment of euthanasia in India today. One is to see if fasting to death has modern relevance in today's world where medical technology keeps people alive for longer and longer periods. Ways of relating the traditional Hindu notion of the religious "good death" with the modern notion of the "meaningful death" are examined. The second is to suggest that, on the evidence of past history, Indian law should not legalize euthanasia, even taking into consideration the new definition of euthanasia which insists on medical diagnosis of terminal disease, due process of decision making, and so forth.

These three case studies in Hindu Ethics demonstrate that Indian thought has not ignored deep reflection on problems which are presenting serious challenges to the modern world. They also demonstrate that Hinduism is more than metaphysics—that it has a firm grounding in ethics even when the most difficult questions are raised.

Notes

1. See, for example, the debates of Rammohun Roy (1772–1833) with the Christian missionaries of his day. An overview is offered by James Pankratz, "Rammohun Roy," as Chapter 7 in *Religion in Modern India*, edited by Robert Baird. New Delhi: Manohar, 1981.
2. P. T. Raju, *Structural Depths of Indian Thought*. Albany: State University of New York Press, 1985.
3. Ibid., p. xvi.
4. Ibid.
5. *Brahmasūtrabhāṣya* Śaṅkara, 1.1.1, as summarized by Karl Potter in *Encyclopedia of Indian Philosophies; Advaita Vedānta up to Śaṃkara and His Pupils*. Princeton: Princeton University Press, 1981, p. 121.
6. Patañjali, *Yoga Sūtras* II.30–32. See translation by J. H. Woods, *The Yoga System of Patañjali*. Delhi: Motilal Banarsidass, 1966.
7. See discussion of Jaimini's *Mīmāṃsāsūtras* by P. T. Raju, *Structural Depths of Indian Thought*, pp. 40–41.

1. Purity in Hinduism: With Particular Reference to Patañjali's Yoga Sūtras

Harold G. Coward

> *There are two widespread pictures of Hindu society in the West. One is of the yogi performing great feats of physical and mental gymnastics, wandering through the world with his begging bowl or sitting motionless in the forest, deep in meditation. The other picture is of the Brahmin priest-scholar at the top of a vast hierarchy of hereditary communities that do not intermarry or even eat together outside the caste. The first picture is supported by the Indian philosophies elaborating various paths that renounce the world and lead to eternal salvation. The second picture has its scriptural support in a different set of sacred texts, the "law books"* (Dharmaśāstras).[1]

The first picture is summed up by the word *mokṣa*—release from the seemingly endless round of death and rebirth. Release, in this picture, is realized by purifying oneself of the pollution created by one's previous births. The second picture is of the caste system guided by the law books and is also very concerned with keeping pure. Purity, then, is a fundamental dimension of all Hindu experience: that of the yogi, the renouncer, and that of the worldly householder. In this chapter, we will comment on how purity functions in both Hindu worlds but will end with our focus on the world of the yogi or renouncer, especially as seen in the fundamental yoga text, *The Yoga Sūtras of Patañjali.* Throughout the chapter, special attention will be given to the ethical impact of purity practices on Hindu women.

The notion of *purity* as somehow being closely related to the *spiritual* has a long history in both the Jewish and Christian traditions. "Cleanliness is next to godliness" was long a motto in the West. Cleanness has a history of being related to holiness. For Christians and Jews to be unclean means to be contaminated by a physical, ritual, or moral impurity.[2] This notion of spiritual purity will provide the Westerner a good beginning point from which to approach Hindu thought and practise and will render understandable even such repulsive behaviour as *satī* or widow burning.

In Hindu Brahmanical culture, the Sanskrit term *śuddha* stands for purity. The meaning of this term in its Hindu usage is best conveyed by invoking images of fullness or completeness in the specific sense of perfection. It refers to the ideal condition of the human body or the most desired state of being. This Hindu notion of purity is effectively summarized as follows:

> *Śuddha* and its opposite *aśuddha* are attributes of animate beings, inanimate objects and places with which a human being comes into contact in the course of everyday life. For example, a prepubescent unmarried girl (*kanyā*), water from a holy river, unboiled milk, ghee and a temple are *śuddha*. On the other hand, contact with certain kinds of human beings (low caste Hindus or non-Hindus), animals (dogs), objects (goods made of leather), foods (beef or food cooked in impure utensils), substances (discharges from a human body), places (cremation ground), etc. causes Brahmans and other upper caste Hindus to become polluted.[3]

Degrees of purity are recognized. Gold, for example, is considered more *śuddha* than copper. Some substances are not only pure in themselves, e.g., water from the Ganges river, but render pure whatever or whosoever comes into contact with them. Thus Ganges water renders the morning bather *śuddha* and is also carried home for cooking and drinking so as to purify one's food and digestive tract. The most pure object for the Brahmin is his three-stranded cotton neck-cord that he wears from the time of his ritual initation onwards. Not only is the neck-cord itself *śuddha,* but when worn it purifies the wearer.

Śauca is a second Sanskrit term which also means *pure.* It functions within the broader context of *śuddha* and relates specifically to ones own personal cleanliness. For instance *Yoga Sūtra* 2.40 describes *śauca* in relation to the cleanliness of one's own body. As the most impure (*aśauca*) substances are the discharges of one's own body. Women, since they have more discharges (e.g., menstruation) than men, are seen as being necessarily more impure. Only in later life, after the menopause, can a woman be seen to approach the standard of *śauca* or purity of a man.

A third Sanskrit term with which we shall have to deal is *sattva. Sattva* is crucial to the Brahmanical sense of superior purity. As we shall see, *sattva* is metaphysically conceived as the pure quality or strand in material nature (*prakṛti*) and is the ideal towards which all purifying practises are directed. Thus it is said that a saintly person is very *sattvic* in quality. The concern of the yogi or the philosopher is usually with the attainment of a spiritual discipline which will so purify one's life as to realize a virtually completely *sattvic* state. It is in such a state, free of pollutions of various kinds, that *mokṣa* or release is realized.

The concern of the Brahmin or Hindu priest and the householder is with a combination of purity and auspiciousness (*śubha*). Just as purity and impurity (*śuddha* and *aśuddha*) is one crucial axis of Hindu life, it is bisected by another equally important axis of auspiciousness and inauspiciousness (*śubha* and *aśubha*). Thus, the situation of the Hindu layperson is most complex. *Śubha* is related to the time at which an event takes place. *Śubha* or auspiciousness is a very complex notion and cannot be examined in detail here.[4] However, the instance of childbirth will provide a good example as to how the pure-impure axis intersects with the auspicious-inauspicious axis. Childbirth is auspicious (*śubha*) if it occurs under the right circumstances defined by the qualities of time, space, and the persons involved, especially the child and the mother. But even if all the circumstances relating to auspiciousness are favourable, the act of childbirth itself, involving as it does the discharge of bodily fluids, renders the mother impure (*aśauca*). The baby is also impure. But this impurity pales into insignificance in the light of the joy of the auspicious character of childbirth, particularly the birth of a son, which is duly celebrated through ritual performance and social ceremonies during the following eleven days, culminating in the ritual of purification. The life of the Hindu householder is rendered most complex by the constant crossing of the purity and auspiciousness axes. It is no wonder, then, that the counsel of a carefully trained priest (Brahmin) is needed to deal successfully with these subtle complexities. A marriage, for example, is a very positive event in that both auspiciousness and purity are judged to be present. By contrast, death is an event involving both pollution and inauspiciousness. But even then some deaths are more inauspicious than others. For example, from the perspective of a wife, it would be much more auspicious if she died being survived by a husband and son. It is very inauspicious for a wife to have her husband die before her, especially if she has no son. To that is added a significant problem of pollution if her husband dies before she has reached the menopause. Thus the terrible prospect of being a young widow in Hinduism—which may have led some to find *satī* (burning to death with the body of one's late husband) preferable to the living of a continually polluted and inauspicious life.

It is the purity side of this complex interrelation of *śuddha* and *śubha* in Hindu life that will be the emphasis of this chapter. And within the purity dimension, more attention will be given to the purity of the yogi or renouncer than the purity of the householder. Early evidence regarding purity will be sampled in the Harappā culture as well as in the Vedas, Epics, and *Laws of Manu*. A survey will be made of purity in worldly life; however, this chapter will focus on the way in which these early ideas are systematized in the *guṇa* theory of Patañjali's *Yoga Sūtras*. The three *guṇas* (*tamas, rajas,* and *sattva*) are described in the *Yoga Sūtras* as having increasing qualities of purity.[5] The purpose of the yoga discipline, outlined by Patañjali, is to purify the *tamas* and *rajas* from one's material nature (*prakṛti*) until one becomes virtually pure *sattva*. In the *Yoga Sūtra* analysis, saliva and bodily discharges are seen as polluting in nature (*tamasic*), and thus the purified yogi shrinks from contact with such substances—even when they are produced by one's own body.[6] Menstruation is seen as very *tamasic*, very polluting. All of this, as will be shown, established a basis for the logical development of a strong negative attitude towards women and towards persons who do not make an effort to practice cleanliness, and are thus empirically seen to be of lower quality (lower caste). Further exemplification of Patañjali's position will be found in the disciplines followed by Gorakhnāth and his followers, the Kānphaṭa Yogis, during the medieveal period. Some implications (e.g., *satī*) for women of the classical Hindu view of purity will be explored. Finally, the clash between the classical view of purity and the negative attitude it established against women and the lower castes will be examined against the background of the equality prescribed by the new Constitution of India.

While this chapter focuses upon the negative value given to the body and its excretions, it must be noted that Hindu thought also includes opposing trends, which place high value upon the body and its fluids. The ambiguous character of bodily fluids in Indian thought will be given some discussion later in the chapter. In the first section Katherine Young's historical discussion of "Women in Hinduism" will provide the overview for my more focused study of purity and impurity in the lives of women.

I. Ancient Indian Ideas about Purity and the Body

In India, some of the most ancient archeological evidence comes from the Harappā city culture on the Indus river 3d to 2d millennium B.C.E.). Cities were fully planned, including sewerage systems. "The houses had bathrooms, the design of which shows that the Harappan, like the modern Indian, preferred to take his bath standing, by pouring pitchers of water over his head."[7] These bathrooms were connected to sewers under the main street which led to soak pits. Of the public buildings, especially in the city Mohenjo Daro, one of the most notable is an oblong bathing pool, thirty-nine by twenty-three feet in area and eight feet deep, constructed of beautiful brickwork. The pool was surrounded by a cloister onto which opened a number of rooms. Basham speculates that, like the bathing pool of a Hindu temple, the Harappā pool probably had a religious purpose. He concludes, "The special attention paid by the people of the Harappā culture to cleanliness is hardly due to the fact that they had notions of hygiene in advance of those of other civilizations of their time, but indicates that, like the latter Hindus, they had a strong belief in the purificatory effects of water from a ritual point of view."[8] Since we still cannot with certainty read the Indus script, we are unable to relate this emphasis on ritual purification to the way in which the Harappā culture viewed the body and its secretions.

Turning to the texts of the Hindus, the most ancient Vedas (1500–500 B.C.E.) give no evidence of a developed dualism of the sort found in the later philosophical speculations—especially those of the Sāṅkhya school where the body is identified with the polluted matter that must be purified. Following Young's analysis in "Women in Hinduism" it may be argued that in the Vedic period, there seems to have been a very positive value given to the woman.[9] Religion was centered in the home and family. A partnership between husband and wife was seen as necessary for the maintenance of order (*ṛta*). This is exemplified in the marriage ceremony described in *Ṛg Veda* 10.58 ff. The bride is described as *jayā* (a sharer of the husband's affections), *janī* (the mother of children), and *patnī* (the partner in the performance of the rituals or *yajña*).[10] The presence of the wife as well as the husband was required for the performance of religious rituals. The partnership of husband and wife provided the context for the fulfillment of earthly life and the atainment of immortality. In addition to the necessary presence of the wife for the performance of *Ṛg Vedic* rituals, there is also evidence that the singing of hymns (*Sāma Veda*) was done by women specially trained in music.[11] Thus, according to Young the *Ṛg Vedic* view was life affirming and family oriented. In it, women had a deep and positive identification with religion. In it, too, the woman as virgin, wife, and mother was deen as pure and auspicious. Indeed, much of the positive self-image of women in India may be traced back to this period.

Although no traces of the later Sāṅkhya doctrine are found in the most ancient Vedic texts, there are beginning speculations which may have prepared the way for the eventual formulation of Sāṇkhya thought. In this regard, special mention may be made of those mythological and cosmological passages emphasizing order and chaos, *sat* and *asat*.[12]

Turning once again to Young's analysis, we find that in the period of the Brāhmaṇas, education shifts from the family home to the home of a specialized teacher. Such teachers had become necessary due to the increasing numbers of hymns and specialization of the ritual. Rather than a simple Vedic ritual done by husband and wife together, the ritual became so complex and complicated that one had to undergo long training to acquire the necessary expertise. In general, it seems that sons, not daughters, went to live with a teacher for this period of extensive study. The *Taittirīya Saṃhitā* VI.3.10.5 says that every Brahmin male had three debts to pay during his life: to repay his debt to the sages, he must live and study with a teacher; to repay his debt to the gods, he must sacrifice; and for the debt to his ancestors, he must produce children, especially sons. Daughters remained at home where they received a brief education but were mainly trained by their mothers for domestic activity. They married older, more mature men who had completed studies with a teacher. Young argues that, the gap between the sexes widened, with women being reduced to being silent partners in ritual activities because they did not have the necessary education. It appears that at the same time the polarity of the pure (*śauca*) and the impure (*aśauca*) became popular as a religious category with women increasingly being viewed as impure, especially at times of menstruation and pregnancy. Because of their lack of knowledge, women (even Brahmin women) were judged *asaṁskṛta* or uncultured and *avaidika* or unlearned. This meant that they were not allowed to go to the assembly, that they must take food after their husbands, that they were powerless, and, indeed, that they were like the Śudras who represented the extreme of being uncultured. Chastity and purity in women came to function as a substitute for the education the men were receiving. As a result, women, although honored for their chastity and purity along with their fertility in producing sons, were at the same time seen as uncultured and unlearned. The positive value of purity was challenged by the greater impurity being ascribed to women at times of menstruation and pregnancy.

When we turn to the later Upaniṣads, clear evidence is found of the beginnings of systematic Sāṅkhya formulation, as well as the negative evaluation of the body and its excretions. It is quite likely that this latter emphasis received at least some stimulus from the very negative Jaina evaluation of the body and its excretions as dark *karma* which weighs down the self and thus must be purged for the self to obtain release.[13]

It is in the *Kaṭha Upaniṣad* that one encounters the first clear outlines of Sāṅkhya dualistic ideas. In the *Kaṭha*, Larsen finds both the old Upanisadic notion of the Self (*ātman*) together with the beginning of the Sāṅkhya notion of an individual self (*puruṣa*).[14] Using the metaphor of the chariot, the *Kaṭha* clearly paves the way for a dualistic analysis of human nature by identifying the Self and its intelligence with the charioteer, while the material nature (mind, sense organs, and objects of the senses) is identified with the chariot and its horses.[15] The Upaniṣad also makes clear that it is the side of the senses and their experiences that must be disciplined and controlled if release is to be achieved.[16] Thus the *Kaṭha*, like the Jainas, suggests that it is the material side of our nature that needs to be purified. In the *Maitrī* and other later Upaniṣads one finds mention of five of the eight *aṅgas* of later classical Yoga; (*prāṇāyāma* or control of breathing; *pratyāhāra* of control of the senses; *dhyāna*, *dhāraṇā* and *samādhi* or increasing degrees of control of the mind).[17] But perhaps of most importance for our analysis of developing ideas relating to purity is *Maitrī's* vivid description of the body as a loathsome conglomerate.

> The body arises from sexual intercourse. It is endowed with growth in darkness [of the womb]. Then it comes forth through the urinary passage. It is built up with bones, smeared over with flesh, covered with skin, filled with faeces, urine, bile, phlegm, marrow, fat, grease and also with many diseases like a treasure house full of wealth.[18]

After this graphic portrait of the polluted nature of the body, the very next verse of the *Maitrī* sets forth descriptions of *tamas* and *rajas*, the qualities that Sāṅkhya and Yoga thought identify as requiring purification.

> Now, it has elsewhere been said: 'The characteristics of the Dark Quality (*tamas*) are delusion, fear, despondency, sleepiness, weariness, heedlessness, old age, sorrow, hunger, thirst, wretchedness, anger, atheism (*nāstikya*), ignorance, jealousy, cruelty, stupidity, shamelessness, religious neglect, pride, unequableness.
>
> The characteristics of the Passionate Quality (*rajas*), on the other hand, are inner thirst, affection, emotion, covetousness, maliciousness, lust, hatred, secretiveness, envy, insatiability, unsteadfastness, fickleness, distractedness, ambitiousness, acquisitiveness, favoritism towards friends, dependence upon surroundings, hatred in regard to unpleasant objects of sense, overfondness in regard to pleasant objects, sourness of utterance, gluttonousness. . . .[19]

The *Maitrī* goes on to add that *sattva* or purity comes from the practice of austerity (*tapas*). This again accords with the Jaina view that the way to purge the heavy *tamasic* and *rajasic karma* from one's self is to starve and burn it out through *tapas*. Another verse quoted in the *Maitrī* identifies impurity with desire.

> The mind is said to be twofold:
> The pure and also the impure
> Impure—by union with desire;
> Pure—from desire completely free![20]

In the *Maitrī*, as in Sāṅkhya, woman sometimes as harlot, is used to symbolize impure desire.[21] And it is equally clear that it is through the practice of purity that release or liberation is achieved: "One should be in a pure place, himself pure (*śuci*), abiding in pureness (*sattva*), studying the Real (*sat*) . . ."[22]

The writers of the Upaniṣads developed an ascetic emphasis. This ascetic thrust polarized desire (*kāma*) over and against control (yoga). For the ascetic woman often came to symbolize desire, the obstacle to release (*mokṣa*). Woman represented sexuality, reproduction, the family, and all of those things that from the ascetic viewpoint functioned as obstacles to release. All of this was mythologically portrayed in stories of celestial nymphs who attempted to seduce ascetics and was sociologically expressed in the ascetics' denial of martial life and concern to retain semen as a source of yogic power.[23]

Let us now turn to Young's analysis of women according to the *smṛti* texts, a vast category of Hindu Sanskrit scripture whose authority is, in theory, secondary to the *śruti* texts of the Vedas.[24] *Smṛti* includes the great epic poems such as the *Mahābhārata* and the *Rāmāyaṇa*, the *Puraṇas*, *Tantras*, and codes of proper behaviour (the *Dharmasūtra* and *Dharmaśāstra*). Woman in these texts are seen as living their lives for the sake of husbands and their children. As a result of being excluded from education during the period of the Brāhmaṇas, women were often rebirth oriented. They were reduced to seeking the spiritual through their husbands, who had knowledge and knew the rituals. Indeed, Hindu women seem to have viewed their husbands as gods or, at least, as channels to the Divine. This tendency, according to Young helps us account for the Hindu woman's ideal of devotion to her husband.[25] According to Young, a woman's devotion to her husband included her offering of well-cooked food, her aesthetics of pleasure, and her production of children. This self-sacrifice of a woman for her husband was understood as a religious offering like that given to the gods. This allowed a woman to spiritualize the mundane aspects of her life.[26] Sometimes a woman would make a special vow (*vrata*) between herself and a god. In such a vow, the woman would voluntarily deny something to herself (e.g., food) in exchange for some favour from the god for her husband (e.g., good health). Through such techniques as vows, women appropriated yogic principles of self-denial into the family setting. The purpose of yogic self-denial of a woman was not direct union with the Divine, as was the case with male yogis, but union with her husband understood as God. In this way, the ascetic ideals of yoga were integrated into the domestic religion of Hindu women.

Young exemplifies this discussion in the portrayal of Sītā, the heroine, in the epic poem, the *Rāmāyaṇa,* with its emphasis on her loyalty, chastity, humility, and strength which arose out of her self-sacrifice (*tapas*) for her husband Rāma.[27] The gist of the story is as follows:

> Rāma, the oldest son and heir to the throne, is banished to the forest as a result of King Daśaratha's fulfillment of a boon to his second wife that her son Bharata be king. Sītā follows her husband Rāma to the forest and

> endures the hardships of forest life. Sītā is abducted by the demon king, Rāvaṇa, and is imprisioned by him on the island of Laṅkā until she is rescued by Rāma. When her fidelity is doubted by the citizens, Rāma, in accordance with sacred law, repudiates her. Sītā proves her chastity by a fire ordeal. After Rāma and Sītā are reunited, they return to Ayodhyā. Bharata renounces the throne and Rāma becomes king.[28]

Sītā is seen by Hindu women as embodying the feminine ideal. This ideal involved much self-sacrifice. When Sītā insisted that she accompany Rāma to the forest, she argued that a woman's place was with her husband, that a wife shared her husband's fortunes and *karma*, that the shade of his feet was greater than all palaces, and furthermore, that she had trained her mind for the hardships of the forest. Her mother-in-law praised this decision as showing that Sītā had overcome the fickleness and weakness of women and that Sītā would aid the spiritual welfare of Rāma. The Epic shows Sītā resorting to austerities, such as vows (*vratas*) and fasting, so as to gain the spirtual strength needed to overcome the obstacles before her. The example of Sītā showed how the Hindu woman, even though reduced to a role of having to approach the Divine through her husband, could still be a pillar of strength in the family.

Turning from Young's discussion of feminine ideals in the *Rāmāyaṇa*, let us sample the *Mahābhārata* and the *Laws of Manu* for ideas relating to purity and the body. In the *Mahābhārata*, a son is a man's own body, while a daughter is bitterest woe.[29] Daughters can attain happiness in heaven only through their sons. A young girl is portrayed as filled with shame on experiencing her first menstrual flow.[30] The *Laws of Manu* strongly reinforce this negative view of menstruation. According to Manu, a menstruating woman is unclean and her presence leaves a noxious stain.[31] The *Mahābhārata* XIII.127.13 even suggests that, should a menstruating woman look at an object, the gods will not take it in sacrifice. Nor can she be in the neighbourhood of the ancestral offering or the forefathers will be unappeased for thirteen years. If a menstruating woman looks at some food, it is unclean and fit only for the demons.[32] This uncleanness associated with the uterus is carried over into the process of conception. According to the *Mahābhārata* XII.213.3ff conception is brought about by seed and blood, is moist with excrement and water, and fouled with the products of blood. These are the constituents of the web of *saṃsāra* or rebirth which desire and the bodies of women spin out. Indeed the very term *rajas* seems to be used in the Epic both for menstrual blood and for desire.[33] The act of intercourse itself is also described by the *Mahābhārata* as unclean.[34] Not surprisingly, the sojourn in the mother's womb is seen as nauseating and gruesome and is described in *Mahābhārata* XII.215.7 as hell's pit (*narakagarta*).

In a more general way, the *Bhagavad-Gītā* teaches that freedom (*mok-*

ṣa) required release from the sway of the three *guṇas*, *sattva* included. This is to be achieved by yoga.[35] In *The Laws of Manu* the *guṇas* are given general descriptions: *sattva* has the form of knowledge; *rajas* of love and hatred and ever draws one toward sensual objects; and *tamas* as darkness, ignorance, delusion, covetousness, and unclean habits.[36]

With this sampling of the *smṛti* texts in regard to purity, the body and women, let us look at Young's summary of the female life cycle from the classical Hindu perspective.[37] Maidenhood, while portrayed by the Sanskrit poets in terms of innocence, charm, and romantic love, was also marked by an obsessive concern on the part of parents to protect the purity of their daughters. Chaste daughters have a very high status in Hindu families and even today (for example during the festival of Durgā Pūjā) are worshipped as the virgin goddess. This stress on chastity led parents to arrange the marriage of their daughters as early as possible. The tendancy toward early marriage was further fostered by the lack of any education for girls. Pushing the marriage forward to the time of puberty or before absolved parents of the responsibility for protecting the girl's chastity. Once married the girl moved in with her husband's family. There she was looked on as a temptress until she bore her first child, preferably a son. Then she was seen as being both safe and auspicious. Over the years, a wife's status increased as long as she had borne at least one son by the time of menopause, when she became asexual like the ascetic. The menopausal woman whose husband had not yet died is judged to have enjoyed the greatest degree of domestic, social, and spiritual freedom of any Hindu woman.[38]

From a woman's perspective, it was auspicious to be survived by one's husband and son or sons. According to Hejib and Young to die before one's husband was not auspicious.[39] It left open two options: to perform *satī* (self-immolation on the funeral pyre of one's husband) or, more commonly, to pass on into widowhood. Whereas *satī* was given a high evaluation (*satī* literally means "good woman"), the widow or *vidhavā* (literally, the one whose husband is dead) was considered not only unfortunate but also inauspicious, especially if she had not yet reached the menopause. Since men were often older than their wives, due to the reasons discussed earlier, this was not infrequently the case. Then, the family not only had an unauspicious widow on its hands but also one who each month produced impurity of a sort that should have been contained and controlled within the context of a living marriage. In addition, the widow herself felt guilty for having failed to ensure the longevity and health of her husband through her vows, sacrifices, and worship (*bhakti*). In this sense, her yoga had been unsuccessful in that her husband had died before her. But, given the presupposition of rebirth, the widow could look forward to reunion with her husband in the next life. So, to purify herself of bad *karma*, which had caused her husband's death, and to produce good *karma* for the next life, the widow spent the remainder of her life in the practice of austerities or *tapas*. She became a female ascetic practising chastity in speech, mind, and deed. She had no possessions (*aparigraha*). She became without desire (*niṣkāma*). She developed endurance and finally developed indifference to all the pairs of opposites (e.g., hot and cold, pleasure and pain, and so on) which characterize our lives. This *tapas* of the widow so purified her that she emerged from her trials serene, radiating benevolence, and eliciting a response of unspoken admiration. Her death was viewed positively as the moment of reunion of husband and wife.

The act of *satī* can also be seen as being directly predicated on the purity ideal. The Vedic basis of *satī* as purifying fire is described as follows:

> *Satī* is a sacrifice by fire. In the *Vedas*, Agni, the god of fire, is said to transfer the substance of the sacrifice and convey this ethereal smoke to the realm of the gods, where it is imbibed by the sense of smell. In later developments of Brahmanism, a purificatory power was attributed to fire, which is important in the rite of *satī*.[40]

In the Hindu view, all death results in pollution for the members of the dead person's family. If there is a widow, this death pollution is focused on her and is removed from the human world by her immolation. For the *satī* to be fully efficacious in removing impurity, it was important that the widow be in as pure a state as possible. Thus there were strict injuctions against *satī* by widows who were menstruating or in a state of birth pollution, for, in these cases, the pollution level of the widow was already such that it would not allow the death pollution to be reduced.[41] Also, before *satī*, the woman's purity was accentuated by a ritual bathing and dressing in new clothes.

According to Hejb and Young when the *satī* state is compared with that of the widow, many similarities emerge. The *satī* engages in a controlled, yoga-like act in entering the fire. In the act of *satī*, she not only burned away her own bad *karma* but also the pollution surrounding the death of her husband. Thus, she purified herself and her family and produced good *karma* for the next life. Her equanimity at the moment of *satī* revealed her yogic attainment.[42] Her act was said to radiate benevolence, not only on the family and those present, but on generations to come. Thus, both the *satī* and the widow perform *tapas* which purifies the pollution of the husband's death and the wife's bad *karma*. The woman choosing *satī* is more auspicious because she instantly reunites herself with her husband. The widow, thinking more of herself, has to use the rest of her own life to put herself back into the state of purity required of being a good wife (*satī*). In addition, the act of *satī* ensured that the couple would be reunited in heaven, while widowhood left open the destination to earth, heaven or hell. Thus, according to Hejib and Young, while the result of *satī* was clear, ambiguity tormented the widow.[43]

Regardless of how they lived or died, one impurity that was inescapable throughout life for the Hindu woman was the pollution of menstruation. Menstruation seems to be regarded as more than a simple physical pollution. In India, menstrual blood has been closely linked with notions of conception. In many texts, there are injunctions to the effect that monthly periods must not be misused that a women's menstruation must be transformed into a fertile result.[44] Some Indian women believe that after ten months of blood is collected, a child is born.[45] Thus fathers who do not provide husbands for their postpubertal daughters are held to commit embryo murder at each menstruation. Husbands also have a duty to have intercourse with their wives at the proper time so that the blood will be used in child production and not issue as menstruation.[46] On the other hand some texts reflect the view of many Hindu women that menstruation is a purifying process. One text says, "Women possess an unrivaled means of purification; they never become entirely foul. For month by month their temporary uncleanness removes their sins."[47] The dominant Hindu view, however, is that menstruation is a pollution.

In the Classical Brahmanical Hindu view, women are assessed and given value in terms of purity. In worldly life, women are seen as existing on a continuum from the most pure as being a prepubertal virgin to the most impure as being a menstruating widow.[48] Since almost the whole of a woman's life seems to caught up in *tamas* or pollution, it is perhaps not surprising that Brahmanical society felt that the desired condition of purity could only be achieved by the imposition of rigorous controls. There is also the concern that the purity of women be maintained to raise the status of their men.[49]

The above discussion has focused on the worldly life picture of Hinduism in which *dharma* is the goal and purity is the means. The pure is noumenal and is symbolised in the *sadhu* or renouncer. The impure is inextricably involved in the cycle of life and death, especially in the case of women. In this impure world, the role of the priest or Brahmin is to help his client maintain or enhance purity. Thus the Brahmin is the exemplar of purity in the world of the nonrenouncers and, as such, sits atop a social hierarchy based on relative purity. As we have seen, this has had a doubly unfortunate effect on the lives of Hindu women. On the one hand it has led to the perception that during menstruation, childbirth, and widowhood they are a major source of pollution, comparable perhaps with that associated with untouchables.[50] In this light, women are seen as of low spiritual value and little social worth. On the other hand, paradoxically, women are also held up as symbols of purity and spiritual power (e.g., Sītā of the *Rāmāyaṇa*). Such women reflect honour upon their menfolk. In a sense, they combine the worship of a pure virgin with that of the reproductive mother.

Sītā was both chaste (and thus pure) and the mother of sons. "Just as purity, virginity and chastity are valued in conformity with caste mores, so too are fertility and maternity valued in conformity with joint family and lineage ideology."[51] For the life-affirming Hindu family, women are a positive and necessary link in the *artha* (acquisition of wealth) chain. Over and against the seeing of women in terms of impurity and chastity, this perspective sees woman as *śakti*, as symbolizing divine creative power. Hinduism has developed the idea of divine motherhood into the idea of cosmic energy (*śakti*) which can be creative, sustaining, or destructive in form. The most developed forms of mother-goddess worship are found among those Hindus who put wordly values to the forefront—typically the Kṣatriya, Vaiśya, and landowning Sūdra. "*Śakti* represents the divine energy in the phenomenal universe, and hence is the chief focus of cult activity on the part of those with materialistic (*artha*) rather than other-worldly (*mokṣa*) or purity (*dharma*) goals."[52] However, this categorization does not always hold. *Śakti,* female power, is experienced by many Hindus as a means not only to material wealth (*artha*) but also as a way of liberation (*mokṣa*). Sometimes in the worship of *śakti,* normal purity and pollution values are turned upside down—as, for example, when sexual intercourse becomes a Tantric practise by which *mokṣa* may be realized. In *bhakti* devotionalism, the sexual relationship between lover and beloved is related to the submissive but passionate relationship between the devotee and the Lord, and is thus transmutted into religious ecstasy and release (*mokṣa*).[53]

Although it is important to note the complex variation in the positive valuations given to sexuality and to women, let us now return to the main analysis of this chapter, namely, the function of purity in Hindu Brahmanical culture. Having surveyed the role of purity and its effect upon women in the worldly or materialistic practise of Hinduism, let us now turn to a detailed examination of purity in that other picture of Hinduism—the picture of the Hindu as the yogi or renouncer. As a method for focusing on the yogi, we will begin by examining ideas relating to purity found in the *Yoga Sūtras of Patañjali.*[54]

II. Purity in the *Guṇa* Theory of Patañjali's *Yoga Sutras*

Patañjali takes the above ideas of the impure nature of the human body, and especially of the womb, and uses them to highlight the nature of human ignorance (*avidyā*). In *Yoga Sūtra* II.5 Patañjali states, *avidyā* is the taking of the impure and highly repulsive body to be pure and attractive. To convince us of the fact that this body (especially of a beautiful, perfumed girl) which seems to us so pure is really full of impurity, Vyāsa in his "commentary" quotes many of the ideas we have encountered earlier:

> Because of its first abode and because of its origin and because of its sustenance and because of its exudations and because of its decease and

> because it needs constant cleaning, the learned recognize that the body is impure.[55]

By way of elucidation, Vacaspati Miśra adds:

> The abode is the mother's womb polluted by such things as urine; the seed is the mother's blood and the father's semen. The sustenance is formation into juices of the food eaten and drunk; for by it the body is held together. Exudation is sweat. And death defiles the body of even a scholarly man. Inasmuch as a bath is required after his dead body is touched.[56]

The body is thus seen as impure in its conception, birth, life, and death. Forgetting about the perfumed girl dominated by desire, even the body of a scholarly man is impure. So for the *Yoga Sūtras*, any body and all its secretions and excretions are thoroughly impure, although in our ignorant infatuation we take such a body to be pure and even beautiful.

Before going on to explain how to deal with this entrapping impurity, Patañjali offers a sophisticated theoretical explanation as to the nature and cause of the impurity. Patañjali, following the Sāṅkhya theory,[57] conceives of consciousness as composed of three aspects of substantive qualities (*guṇas*): *sattva* (brightness, illumination, intelligence), *rajas* (emotion, activity), and *tamas* (dullness, inertia). Although each of these *guṇas* keeps its own separate identity, no individual *guṇa* ever exists independently. Rather, the three *guṇas* are always necessarily found together like three strands of a rope. However, the proportionate composition of consciousness assigned to each of the *guṇas* is constantly changing.[58] Only the predominate *guṇa* will be easily recognized in a particular thought, perception, or material structure. The other two *guṇas* will be present but subordinate, and therefore their presence will have to be determined by inference. If a psychological cross section were taken through an ordinary state of consciousness, there would be a dominance of *tamas* and *rajas* especially in its evolved forms of ego, sense organs, and their everyday experiences. In our routine states of consciousness and bodily experience, there is a noticeable lack of *sattva* or pure discriminative awareness. It is for this reason that we habitually make the error described in *Yoga Sūtra* II.5 of taking the impure body to be pure. In *guṇa* terms, the body is dominated by *tamas* and *rajas*. Only when our sense organs and mental states (*citta vrittis*) are purified of domination by the passion and desire of *rajas* are they pure enough to allow us to see the body for the impure thing it is. According to Patañjali, it is by following the practices set forth in the *Yoga Sūtra* that the proportionate composition of the mental states is reversed with *sattva* becoming dominant over *rajas*. At its height, a pure *sattva* experience would be like the direct transparent viewing of reality with no emotional (*rajas*) or bodily (*tamas*) distortion intervening. This is technically termed *nirvicārasamādhi* and is defined as a supernormal perception that transcends the ordinary categories of time, space, and causality and has the capacity to directly "grasp" or "see" the real nature of things.[59] It is this pure *sattva* intuition which is given detailed analysis in *Sūtras* I.41–51 of the *Yoga Sūtras* that provides the criterion for purity against which the ordinary body is judged to be impure.

The purpose behind the evolving nature of the *guṇas*, and the desire of the *Yoga Sūtras* for their increasing purification, is to enable the True Self (*puruṣa*) to be seen. Ordinarily we take our body and its desires to be the locus of our True Self. But the experience of Patañjali and the other great yogis is that the taking of the body with its dominating *tamas* and *rajas* constituents to be the locus of the True Self is an error. Only when the impure *tamas* and *rajas* are purged through the practice of the yoga disciplines (the *yogāṅgas*) do the body and the mental states become sufficiently transparent (*sattva*) to enable one to experience one's True Self as *puruṣa* (inner spirit), rather than as the material states of one's mind and body (*prakṛti*).[60] To use the analogy of the light bulb and lampshade, *puruṣa*, the True Self, is like a pure shining light (with its own power source) within each of us, while *prakṛti*, the body, sense organs, and mental states (composed of the three *guṇas*), is like the lampshade. When *prakṛti* (the lampshade) is purified of darkness (*tamas*) and passionate activity (*rajas*), it becomes transparent (*sattva*), and we discover ourselves to be not a passionate body and mind but a *puruṣa* of pure intelligent consciousness. Lest the puritan attitude and practice of Patañjali's Yoga be misunderstood, it is important to keep in mind that it is this ultimate purpose of release from ignorance into true self-knowledge (the Yoga parallel to salvation) that drives the desire for the purification of body and mind.

Aside from the above description of the nature of the impurity in terms of the three *guṇas*, the cause of the impurity is given further analysis in *Yoga Sūtra* II.15 in terms of the action of *karma*. *Karma* is described by Patañjali as a memory trace recorded in the unconscious by any action or thought a person has done. The Westerner should especially note that, for Yoga, a thought is as real as an action—in fact, in the Yoga view, we think first and then act, and thought therefore is of primary psychological importance. The *karmic* memory trace (*saṁskāra*) remains in the unconscious as a predisposition towards doing the same action or thought again in the future. All that is required is that the appropriate set of circumstances present themselves, and the *karmic* memory trace, like a seed that has been watered and given warmth, bursts forth as an impulsion toward the same kind of action or thought from which it originated. If one, through the exercise of free choice, chooses to act on the impulse and do the same action or thought again, then that *karmic* seed is allowed to flower, resulting in a reinforcing of the memory trace within the unconscious. Sufficient repetitions of the same action or thought produce a strengthening of the predisposition (*saṁskāra*) and the establishing of a habit pattern or *vāsanā*. Such a *karmic* habit pattern or *vāsanā* is the Yoga equivalent for the modern psychological notion of motivation.[61] The unconscious, in yoga terminology, is nothing more than the sum total of all stored up *karmic* traces from the thoughts and actions done in this and previous lives. Bad *karmic* habits, such as not bathing, not washing and preparing food properly, giving in to base and materialistic desires, and the ego pursuit of one's own fame and fortune, all serve to colour one's lampshade with darker hues so that the true self (*puruṣa*) is not seen. In the yoga view, the ordinary experience of all of us is to take our true nature to be our body and mind dominated by the darker *karma* of our desires—desires predisposed by our desiring in past lives. It is this lampshade of dark *karma* that prevents us from seeing the lightbulb of our pure *puruṣa* within and that causes us to mistakenly think of our impure bodies and minds as pure.

The "Commentary" on *Yoga Sūtra* II.15 describes all of this in vivid detail. In every experience of pleasure, the mind and the body are permeated with passion (*rajas*) leaving behind a latent deposit of *karma*. Pain also causes a passionate response and similarly leaves behind a latent deposit of *karma*. A further and more subtle kind of *karma* is the frustration that results from the cessation of a pleasurable experience—we are always left wanting more of food, drink, sex, material possessions, and so forth. Thus, even our experiences of mental and bodily pleasure, on analysis, are seen to predispose us to future similar acts and necessarily to end in painful frustration. This is the beginningless stream of our ordinary experience, which causes the impurity of mind and body and blocks our true perception of the pure *puruṣa*. While being immersed in all of this impurity does not bother the average person, to the one who has begun to purify mind and body through the practice of yoga and who has begun to see these *karmic* impulses (*saṁskāras*) for what they are, such *saṁskāras* are felt by the yogi to be as painful as if they were a wool thread being pulled across the eyeball. It is precisely this extreme sensitivity that causes the yogi to withdraw from contact with anything representing the heavier *karma* which causes this pain, e.g., impure food, unwashed bodies, the bodies and minds of those whose habits are marked by *rajasic* and *tamasic karma*, and finally to shrink from contact even from one's own body. This condition is the basic prerequisite requirement for beginning the practice of yoga. It is nicely summarized in the Comment on *Yoga Sūtra* II.1:

> Yoga is not attained by one not given to purificatory action. Impurity is variegated by the eternal in-dwelling of the aroma of action and affliction [the unconscious karmic impulses, *vāsanās*], and is ever in contact with the network of enjoyables. It cannot be dispersed without purificatory action (*tapas*).[62]

Vyāsa goes on to add that, in addition to purifactory action, study or the repeated utterance of purifying words like AUM and making Iśvara the motive of all ones actions are to be practiced by the yogi. Let us now examine these prescriptions for purifying the mind and body in more detail.

Śaucha or cleanliness is one of the *aṅgas* or means to yoga by which impurity can be removed and discriminative awareness of *puruṣa* realized. Vyāsa in his Commentary on *Yoga Sūtra* II.32 defines *śaucha* as cleanliness of two kinds: external and internal. External cleanliness involves washing of the body by earth and water. External cleanliness also includes the eating of pure food, properly washed and prepared. Tradition adds that, to be pure, food must not contain meat, fish, or eggs and must not be touched by saliva or by the left hand (used to perform ablutions).[63] To these requirements the Hatha Yogis add various practices designed to clean the digestive tract, e.g., fasting, passing a strip of cloth into the stomach, and sitting in a tub of water to give oneself an enema.[64] Internal cleanliness involves the washing of impure thoughts such as arrogance, pride and jealousy from the mind. The test for mastery of cleanliness is most revealing for the point being made in this study. In *Yoga Sūtra* II.40 Patañjali states, "As a result of cleanliness there is disgust at one's own body and no intercourse with others."[65] The practice of purity of body and mind leads the yogi to be disgusted and shrink from contact, not only with the bodies of others, but even from his own body and its excretions. Vyāsa comments:

> As soon as there is disgust with his own body, he [the yogi] has begun cleanliness. Seeing the offensiveness of the body, he is no longer attached to the body and becomes an ascetic (*yati*). Moreover there is no intercourse with others. Perceiving the true nature of the body, even after he has washed it with earth and water and other substances, not seeing any purity in the body, how could he have intercourse with the bodies of others absolutely unhallowed as they are?[66]

In terms of the *guṇa* theory, this means that the body is composed of *karmic* impurities of the nature of *rajas* and *tamas*. To be clean (*sattvic*) requires ultimately that one get rid of one's body and impure thoughts. Implied in the text is that the further one departs from the relatively pure practice and body of the yogi, the more revolting (*tamasic*) the bodies of others become. There is even the implication that these darker qualities can rub off from the body and mind of another onto oneself. Thus all contact with others is to be avoided, especially with those who are not even trying to be clean—those who eat meat, don't wash properly, indulge in sexual intercourse, and engage in uncouth activity not only in this life but also in previous lives. The most likely candidates for this latter group in Indian society are of course the lower castes and classes. The yogi, like the Brahmin, is one who has worked hard at purifying body and mind not only in this life but likely also in previous lives. It is simply not good either for the individual's spiritual progress or the well-being of society to lose such purity by contact with those who, due to their own free choice (after all according to Patañjali's theory they created their own *karma*), are more impure. As Arjuna puts it (speaking in another context):

> The mixing of caste leads to hell,—[the hell] prepared for those who wreck the family and for the family [so wrecked]. So too their ancestors fall down [to hell], cheated of their offerings of food and drink.[67]

All of this provides an excellent basis for the development of a negative attitude toward others of a lower *karmic* level than oneself—those not practising yoga, people of lower castes, and cetainly people who live outside of the caste structure, the untouchables. This negative attitude is not based on any dislike for others. In Patañjali's view, it is simply a recognition of the fact that to achieve release from rebirth (*saṁsāra*) one must become *sattvic* in body and mind. That, in turn, requires the avoidance of contact with others, especially those grossly impure, and eventually even with one's own body. From this perspective, women at all levels of caste purity are more repulsive than men because their bodies produce more polluting excretions, i.e., menstruation. As we have already noted in discussion of *Yoga Sūtra* II.5, the symbol of impurity given the text is a woman's body and particularly her womb.

In addition to the practice of internal and external cleanliness, the *Yoga Sūtra* II.32 also requires *tapas*. Although virtually untranslatable, *tapas* is the yogic practice of forcefully exposing oneself to physical suffering in the face of the pairs of opposities (*dvandva*) such as heat and cold, hunger and thirst, standing and sitting. By meditating at the height of summer surrounded by bonfires, the yogi was thought to expose the dark *tamas* and *rajas* to a kind of "intense white heat" that rapidly burned up such polluting qualities. *Yoga Sūtra* II.43 suggests that such *tapas* "in the very act of completing itself destroys defilement from the covering of impurity."[68] Vyāsa adds that through such intense purification of the body achieves the power of atomization (described in *Yoga Sūtra* III.45), and the sense organs, by virtue of their *sattvic* transparency, the ability to see and hear at a distance, i.e., telepathy.

The goal of the yogic practice of cleanliness and *tapas* is to free oneself from the polluting sway of the *guṇas*. Vacaspati Miśra describes it clearly in his "Explanation" on *Yoga Sūtra* I.16, "The purity of knowledge consists in the steady flow of the quality of essence (*sattva*), due to the removal of active disturbance (*rajas*) and inertia (*tamas*). This brings about recognition of the distinct natures of the *puruṣa* and the 'qualities.'"[69] Vyāsa makes clear that both the body and the mental states have been purified of *karma* and the dark *guṇas*. Indeed, the purity attained is such that the mind has become like a transparent crystal which clearly reflects what is placed before it.[70] Once the concentration of the yogi is turned inward upon the flow of consciousness itself, what is seen is *puruṣa*, the true Self, since all other *karmic* obscurations have been purged from both body and mind.[71] While all of this yogic achievement is admirable from the point of view of its spiritual goal, a direct result of the *guṇa* theory employed is a very negative view of those persons who do not practise yoga, who are of the lower castes, or who happen to be women. This negative view is a most unfortunate flip side of the purity which the yogi struggles so hard to achieve.

III. Further Exemplification of Patañjali's Position in the Disciplines of Gorakhnāth and His Followers

The ancient Indian ideas regarding purity and the body found in the Vedas and latter systematized in Sāṅkhya and Yoga theory are further exemplified in the Kānphaṭa Yogis of the medieval period. The Kānphaṭa Yogis look upon Gorakhnāth as the founder of their order. Traditions and legends concerning Gorakhnāth are widespread in India through Nepal, the United Provinces, Bengal, Western India, and the Punjab. Gorakhnāth is looked on as more than a human teacher. He is thought of as being outside the ordinary laws of time and appearing on the earth in different ages or *yugas*. He is said to have lived in the Punjab, and historical references would place his date not later than 1200 C.E.[72] Gorakhnāth seems to have been the author of the *Gorakṣaśataka*, a mingling of Yoga and Tantra doctrines. Many of its verses are copied verbatim in the later *Haṭhayogapradīpika* of Savātmārāma. These two texts are foundational for the practice of the medieval yogis.[73]

In the *Gorakṣaśataka*, as is the case in Patañjali's Yoga, special attention is paid to the power of breath (*prāṇa*) and its regulation. The body is thought of as filled with *nāḍis*, which are conceived of as subtle channels of power having their ends or outlets in the openings of the body.[74] The aim of the yoga practice is to purify these channels so that the breath or *prāṇa* can pass through them freely. In our ordinary state, the channels are conceived of as full of impure secretions. As the *Haṭhayogapradīpika* puts it:

> The Nādis should be cleansed of their impurities by performing the mudrās, etc. (which are the practices relating to the air) āsanas, kumbhakas and various curious mudrās.[75]

Some of the more unusual of these practices include: *dhauti* (slowly swallowing and drawing out a long narrow wet rag), *vasti* (sitting in a tub of water and giving oneself an enema by inserting a small bamboo tube into the anus), *neti* (inserting a smooth nine inch thread in through a nostril and out through the mouth), and *gajakaraṇi* (self-induced vomiting to clean out the stomach). To these are added many yogic postures, each designed to purify some organ or channel of the body.[76] All of these practices are aimed at cleaning out impurities (food, faeces, phlegm, mucous secretions, and so on) so that the breath or *prāṇa* flows freely through the subtle channels or *nāḍis* of the body. When the channels have been cleansed, the body is said to become lean and of a glowing colour, the appetite is strong, youth is regained, divine sounds are heard, and the power of death may be destroyed.[77] Once the *nāḍis* are cleaned, the way is open for the arousal of the great power (*kuṇḍalini*) by the practice of *prāṇa* until the final state of spiritual knowledge (*jñāna*) or release (*mukti*) is realized.[78] Rather than totally ridding oneself of the body, as was the goal with Patañjali, Gorakhnāth's aim is for a perfectly purified divine body. As he puts it in his *Gorakṣaśataka*, verse 101:

> By cleansing the nāḍis the prāṇa is restrained as desired, the digestive fire is kindled, internal sound is heard, and one becomes diseaseless.[79]

Having this outline of Gorakhnāth's yoga in mind, let us examine the implications of this particular emphasis on purification for the attitude toward women.

In Gorakhnāth's *Gorakṣaśataka*, the ordinary state of the body is that the *nāḍis* are full of impure secretions.[80] The aim is the drying up of the liquids of the body.[81] Since women's bodies—by virtue of menstruation and giving birth—have more secretions, they are judged to be more impure than the ordinary bodies of men. Indeed, the notion of *rajas* is carried over from Sāṅkhya and Yoga and defined by Gorakhnāth as menstrual fluid.[82] The goal is to dry up and withdraw the *rajas*, thus, in a sense, achieving a reversal of nature. Since women are the embodiment of the usual course of nature and the supreme temptation to continue in it, they are judged by Gorakhnāth and his followers as the greatest impediment in one's progress towards immortality.[83] In the Nāth literature, woman is depicted as the tigress from whom man must save himself. Charmed and allured by her, the man looses vital energy. She is the enchantress of the day and tigress of the night. The Nāth yogis were strict celibates. For them, pleasure in the company of women leads inevitably to death, forsaking women leads to life.[84] The Nāths regarded women as the greatest danger on the path to yoga. They are given the status of ferocious tigresses bent on sucking the blood of the prey. Gorakhnāth himself is reported to have said, "The breath of women dries up the body and youth vanishes day by day. Foolish are the people who understand nothing and make pets of tigresses in everyhouse; in the day the tigress becomes the world-enchantress and at night she dries up the whole body."[85] In the Nāth literature women are generally termed as thieves, dacoits, pirates, thirsty tigresses and hypocrite cats.[86]

In the physiology of the day, this drying up of the male body is understood in a very literal way: the emission of semen in sexual intercourse was understood to be a loss of the male's vital energy—energy essential for the practice of yoga. Thus, some of the more esoteric yoga practices were aimed at saving the male seed (the *mahā-rasa*) from any kind of discharge, even in the alluring presence of women. This was especially true for the precursors of the Nāth Yogis, the Sahajiyā yogis who needed the help of a woman for the practice of their yoga. The Sahajiyā yogis followed the Tantric technique of joining with a woman in intercourse after having completely mastered the temptation she offered. Most often the woman is only present in the mind, as a part of the meditative exercise—the *śakti* or female force of nature.[87] In some cases, however, the intense emotion of the physical experience of intercourse was used to induce the deeper experience of being carried out of oneself and into divine bliss.[88] The status of the woman engaged in such yogic practice is unclear. Sometimes she seems to have been seen as participating in the spirituality of the experience, while at other times she is treated simply as a sexual object—a low caste, polluted harlot or washerwoman from outside the city (a *dombī*) who was engaged for the purpose. But even the few Sahajiyā yogis who would allow such practices were very aware of the dangers introduced by intimate involvement with a woman.

Wendy O'Flaherty has noted that, in post-Vedic India, menstrual blood has an ambiguous character. In some Tantric rituals, mentrual blood is eaten. Sometimes menstrual blood is seen as nonpolluting, as being the female creative power (parallel to the male semen) and, as such, sacred or taboo. In post-Vedic mythology, menstrual blood sometimes appears as a symbol of the passion of women—as their fertile erotic fluid.[89] In the primative physiology, menstrual blood, rather than the ovum, was taken to be the female component which combined with the male semen to produce conception. Sometimes milk is described as being made from menstrual blood—the most polluting of substances becomes the purest of substances.[90]

It is evident in the above paragraphs that a secondary tradition in Hindu India sees females and their body fluids as at times positive and powerful. However, even in this secondary Tantric tradition, the fluids within the body are basically a pernicious force which needs to be controlled.[91] The rules set forth in the *Dharmaśāstras* reflect the mainstream of Hindu thinking on how to keep the bodily fluids flowing (a necessity for the householder life) in ways that will do the least damage.

Many of the stories of the great yogis of India include a fall at the hands of a tempting woman.[92] It is of interest to note that, in this literature, Mayanāmatī, one of the few women to reach the status of the yogic hero, is given mixed reports. Although given initiation by none other than Gorakhnāth, himself, some reports suggest that her conduct was not above suspicion—even though she denied any misbehavior (all this recalls to mind the experience of Sītā, the heroine of the *Rāmāyaṇa*). While depicted as a woman of mystic wisdom (a Tantric *ḍakinī*) in the Nāth literature, Mayanāmatī has also been regarded as someone with supernatural powers midway between a witch and a goddess.[93]

Research is needed to explore the situation of other women who achieved the high status of being acclaimed yogic heroes. Ānandamayī Mā is a recent example. In his study of her life, Alexander Lipski reports that, for her, the question of sexual desire did not even arise. Nor was her marriage ever physically consummated. When her husband, Bholānāth, first tried to approach her physically he is reported to have received such a violent electric shock from her body that he quickly lost all desire. On other occasions when sexual desire entered even his unconscious mind, Mā's body is said to have assumed all the symptoms of death, quashing Bholānāth's sexual desire and causing him to become frightened and chant *mantras* as a way of reestablishing contact with his wife. She quickly became his *guru* or spiritual master, and the remainder of their life together functioned in the *guru*-student relationship in which all feeling was spiritual rather than sexual.[94] No evidence is offered as to whether her menstrual flow dried up (at a young age) under the influence of her spiritual *sādhanā*. Such an outcome would not be unexpected given that menstruation can be inhibited by strong psychic states (e.g., mental stress). Such a lack of menstruation in one such as Ānandamayī Mā would fit in well with Patañjali's notion of a *sattvic* dominance of mind and body.

Returning to the Nāth Yogis, the followers of Gorakhnāth, it is clear that for them, as for Patañjali, women are viewed negatively. While caste is overcome in that Nāth Yogis have no caste and all eat together, their women are not allowed to eat with them.[95] Some women are given initiation. They are either married women or those who enter the sect after the death of their husbands.[96] Although such initiation gave women a higher status than they received elsewhere in medieval India,[97] they were still in the position of being very much second class citizens. Certainly at least until the menopause, a women's body was necessarily more polluted than the body of a man. In their ascetic orders, the Nāth nuns were governed by monks. The subordination of the nuns was due to their more polluted physiological state. For the Nāth Yogis, as for Patañjali, the simple fact of human nature was that women, because of their greater degrees of bodily secretion, embodied more *rajas* and *tamas*. Consequently, they were more polluted, a source of temptation to the yogi and thus to be avoided.

IV. The Clash Between the Classical View of Purity and the Equality Prescribed by India's New Constitution

The classical Indian view—that low caste and femaleness is simply a reflection of the *karma* one had established for oneself due to one's own free choices in previous births—is rejected in the thought of contemporary Hindu thinkers and in the provisions of India's Constitution. One modern Hindu writer, Swami Iśwarananda, criticizes the classical view of *karma* and rebirth as having produced a certain callousness towards others—their needs and situation in life. The point Iśwarananda makes is that *karma* theory implies that it is inappropriate or even hopeless to attempt to ameliorate situations of distress or injustice in the human community. As he puts it,

> the prevalent Hindu doctrine that one's life is solely determined by one's karma and therefore one can afford to be callous toward the suffering of those around him has been responsible for not only the neglect of the masses in India by the aristocracies of learning, power and wealth, but also for standing as a barrier to their growth and welfare.[98]

The application of these remarks to the lack of equality experienced by low castes and women in the classical *karma* and *guṇa* theory is obvious. Another modern thinker, Sanat Kumar Sen, states the problem is a less polemic fashion: ". . . the assumption of Karma may even seem to justify callousness in the face of human suffering, for if everybody's fate is a result of his own action, why should we attempt to mitigate others' miseries except on the grounds of selfishness."[99] Other writers, of course, deny that such a selfish result is entailed by the doctrine of *karma*, emphasizing the individual's present freedom to act in morally responsible ways as provided for by *karma* and *guṇa* theory.[100] One modern Hindu who stressed the freedom present in classical *karma* theory even to the point of social revolution was Swami Vivekananda. Vivekananda went so far as to use *karma* theory as a basis to criticize the oppressed for their weakness. The following story was retold within the Ramakrishna Order.

> It was in Almora that a certain elderly man, with a face full of amiable weakness, came and put him a question about Karma. What were they to do, he asked, whose Karma it was to see the strong oppress the weak? The Swami turned on him in surprise indignation. "Why, thrash the strong, of course!" he said, "You forget your own part in this Karma; Yours is always the right to rebel."[101]

For Vivekananda, *karma* has manufactured your body and mind for you. What you do with its future possibilities is up to you. While it is true that *karma* theory, as systematized by Patañjali, does stress that *karmic* impulses are merely dispositions from past actions, not predeterminations, still one cannot avoid the fact that the *guṇa* theory and its sense of the physical reality of impurity leads one to shrink from contact with others—especially low caste persons and menstruating women. Some modern writers feel that, with the advent of modern scientific knowledge, *karma* theory is no longer acceptable. As Sarasvati Chennakesavan puts it, "With the spread of scientific and technological knowledge, an explanation for the physiological and mental inequalities so far-fetched as the *karma* theory has become unacceptable. Facts of sociological economics and social psychology combined with anthropology are able to explain inequalities that so puzzled our ancestors."[102] What Chennakesavan and most other modern writers fail to address is the spiritual motivation behind the classical ideas—a motivation that can still capture the modern scientific mind, as witnessed by the appeal of Patañjali's Yoga for well-educated Westerners.

A major conflict exists between the presupposition of the classical view and that of the Constitution of India adopted in 1949. The Preamble of the Constitution resolves to secure to all its citizens justice, liberty, equality, and fraternity, assuring the dignity of the individual and the unity of the nation.[103] Part III of the Constitution entitled "Fundamental Rights" leads off with a section on "The Right to Equality." In this section, provision 15(1) states "The State shall not discriminate against any citizen on grounds only of religion, race, caste, sex, place of birth or any of them." Provision 15(2) goes on to elaborate that no citizen shall be subject to any disability, limitation, or restriction in terms of access to public buildings (including Hindu Temples); to the use of wells, tanks, bathing *ghats*, roads, or public resorts; or to be discriminated against in respect of employment. The two main groups in mind here are women and those of low caste. This is made clear by sections of provision 15 which allow the state to set up special conditions for the advancement of women and low caste groups without violating the requirement for equality of treatment. Provision 16 deals with "Untouchability," which it abolishes. All these provisions directly attack the gradations of individuals and groups which was the natural result of the classical *guṇa* theory and its view of the body, especially the female body, as being filled with impurities. Whereas before the Constitution, and in line with the classical view, the untouchable could bring merchandise only as far as the back gate. Only after the untouchable deposited whatever it was at the back gate and physically removed his polluting presence could the pure Brahmin come out of the house to pick up the delivery. Even then the object, whatever it was, would have to be thoroughly washed before being taken into the house. Similarly, in the house, the women had to keep apart from the presence of the men, eating and sitting separately.

The Constitution not only attempted to reject these negative attitudes based on the classical view of purity, it also forcefully opposed them by strongly stating the rights to freedom for all as including freedom of speech, of assembly, of movement, of settling, of holding property, and of practising and profession, see 19(1).

In his study of the Constitution and the secular India it seeks to establish, D. E. Smith observes that the above provisions constitute a revolution in the traditional conception of religion in India.[104] The revolution that the Constitution introduces is nothing short of a new standardization of Hindu personal law on the basis of equality rather than on the classical view of *karmic* purity. On the new basis of equality, women are no longer to be seen as inferior to men by virtue of their greater bodily impurity. Nor are people who eat meat or engage in sex and worldly pleasures to be judged as inferior to the ascetic yogis by virtue of the impurity of their lifestyles. Indeed, the very idea of ordering society in terms of levels of purity and impurity, which, in part at least produced the caste system, is ruled out by the new Constitution. These equality provisions of the Constitution have also provided the basis for legislation opening Hindu religious institutions to all classes and sections of India. Harijan temple entry laws have been enacted by many state legislatures. "The central Untouchability (Offenses) Act of 1955 provides *inter alia* that any attempt to prevent Harijans from exercising their right of temple entry is punishable with imprisonment, fine or both."[105] Court interpretations of the equality provisions of the Constitution have quashed attempts of a religious community to excommunicate one of its members, thus highlighting the clash between the role of the state and its equality provisions with the internal autonomy of a religious demonination.[106] While excommunication in the West is mainly a matter of religious belief, in India excommunication exists much more on the social level as an act of removing a person from a particular caste group or baring the entry of others into a particular caste. The roots of such discrimination are found in the classical views of religious purity as sanctification. The outlawing of excommunication by the courts is a dramatic example of the clash between the egalitarian philosophy of the Constitution and the elitist (by one's own efforts) approach of Hindu *karma* and *guṇa* theory. What the Constitution does not address, of course, is whether the provision of equality is true and just, whereas the Hindu distinctions made on the basis of *karmic* purity in search of *mokṣa* are to be overturned as untrue and unjust. The basis of the ancient Hindu views of purity are found in the *śruti* and *smṛti* which, for the Hindu, have the status of revelation. What makes the modern situation especially ambiguous is that the Constitution sees itself as providing freedom of religion, on the one hand, and yet removes that freedom when the basic revelations of the religion are found to contravene the Constitution's premise of equality. The courts of India have the difficult task of having to arbitrate this fundamental clash.[107]

Notes

1. John B. Carman, "Axes of Sacred Value in Hindu Society," in *Purity and Auspiciousness in Indian Society,* edited by John B. Carman and Frederique A. Marglin. Liden: E. J. Brill, 1985, p. 109.
2. "Clean and Unclean", *The Interpreter's Dictionary of the Bible,* vol. 1, New York: Abingdon Press, 1962, pp. 641ff.
3. T. N. Madan, "Concerning the Categories *śubha* and *śuddha* in Hindu Culture" in *Purity and Auspiciousness in Indian Society,* p. 17.
4. For an excellent analysis see the papers by T. N. Madan, A. Hillebeitel, V. Narayan, and F. A. Marglin in *Purity and Auspiciousness in Indian Society,* 1985.
5. *Yoga Sūtra* I.2
6. *Yoga Sūtra* 2.32 on *śaucha.*
7. A. L. Basham, *The Wonder That Was India.* New York: Grove Press, 1959, p. 16.
8. Basham, *The Wonder That Was India,* p. 18.
9. Katherine Young, "Hinduism" in *Women in World Religions,* edited by Arvind Sharma, Albany, New York: State University of New York Press, 1987, pp. 59–103.
10. Shakuntala Rao Sastri, *Women in the Vedic Age.* Bombay: Bharatiya Vidya Bhavan, 1969, p. 16.
11. Bhagwat Saran Upadhaya, *Women in Ṛgveda.* New Delhi: S. Chand & Co., 1974, p. 185.
12. See the analysis of Gerald Larsen, *Classical Sāṅkhya.* Delhi: Motilal Banarsidass, 1979, p. 94. Some scholars, however, question this analysis by Larsen.
13. See Padmanabh S. Jaini, *The Jaina Path of Purification.* Berkeley: University of California Press, 1979, Cp IV "The Mechanism of Bondage."
14. Larsen, *Classical Sāṅkhya,* p. 97, for his analysis of the *Kaṭha Upaniṣad.*
15. *Kaṭha Upaniṣad* III.3–4.
16. *Kaṭha Upaniṣad* III.6 & V.1.
17. See Mircea Eliade, *Yoga: Immortality and Freedom.* Princeton: Princeton University Press, 1969, p. 25.
18. *Maitrī Upaniṣad* III.4 as translated by S. Radhakrishnan, *The Principal Upaniṣads.* London: Allen and Unwīn, 1968, p. 807.
19. *Maitrī Upaniṣad* III.5 as translated by R. E. Hume, *The Thirteen Principal Upanisads.* Oxford: Oxford University Press, 1968, pp. 419–420.

20. *Maitrī Upaniṣad,* as quoted in VI.34, trans. by R. E. Hume.
21. *Maitrī Upaniṣad* VI.10.
22. *Maitrī Upaniṣad* VI.30, trans. by R. E. Hume.
23. Katherine Young, "Hinduism," in *Women in World Religions*, p. 70.
24. Katherine Young, "Hinduism", pp. 72–92. For a detailed analysis of *śruti* and *smṛti* texts and their function as Hindu scripture, see Harold Coward, *Sacred Word and Sacred Text: Scripture in World Religions.* Maryknoll, New York: Orbis Books, 1988.
25. See Katherine Young, "Hinduism" for a detailed analysis of this development, pp. 73f.
26. Alaka Hejib and Katherine K. Young, "Power of the Meek (*abalā*): A Feature of Indian Feminism." Unpublished paper presented to the American Academy of Religion, New Orleans.
27. See Katherine Young, "Hinduism," p. 78.
28. Romesh C. Dutt, *The Ramayana and the Mahabharata.* New York: Everyman's Library, 1969.
29. *Mahābhārata* XII.243.20 as quoted by Johann Jakob Meyer, *The Sexual Life of Ancient India.* Delhi: Motilal Banarsidass, 1971, p. 7.
30. *Mahābhārata* III.303 ff.
31. "The Sacred Books of the East," *The Laws of Manu,* trans. by G. Bühler, vol. 25, Delhi: Motilal Banarsidass, 1967, vol. XI, pp. 171–174.
32. Meyer, *The Sexual Life of Ancient India,* p. 225.
33. Ibid, p. 362.
34. Ibid, pp. 240–241.
35. T. R. V. Murti, "The Gitā-Conception of Philosophy and Religion," in *Studies in Indian Thought,* edited by Harold Coward. Delhi: Motilal Banarsidass, 1983, p. 313.
36. *The Laws of Manu,* XII.24–37.
37. This summary is taken from Katherine Young, "Hinduism," pp. 80ff.
38. James M. Freeman, "The Ladies of Lord Krishna: Rituals of Middle-Aged Women in Eastern India," *Unspoken Worlds: Women's Religious Lives in Non-Western Cultures,* ed. Nancy Auer Falk and Rita M. Gross. San Francisco: Harper and Row, 1980, p. 126.
39. Alaka Hejib and Katherine K. Young, "Towards Recognition of the Religious Structure of the Sati." Paper presented to the American Oriental Society, 1978. The following description of the widow is taken from this article as cited by Katherine Young, "Hinduism," pp. 83–86.
40. Elizabeth Leigh Stutchbury, "Blood, Fire and Meditation: Human Sacrifice and Widow Burning in Nineteenth Century India" in *Women in India and Nepal,* ed. Michael Allen and S. N. Mukherjee. Canberra: Australian National University, 1982, p. 23. Stutchbury offers accounts of both voluntary and non-voluntary *satī.*

41. Ibid, p. 36.
42. One eyewitness report describes such stoicism of the *satī* in the fire as follows: "I stood near enough to touch the pile, but I heard no sound and saw no motion, except one gentle upheaving of the brushwood over the body after which all was still." Ibid., p. 32.
43. Katherine Young, "Hinduism," p. 85.
44. Jocelyn Krygier, "Caste and Female Pollution," in *Women in Nepal and India*, p. 77.
45. Ibid.
46. Ibid.
47. Ibid., p. 94. The quote is from Baudhayana II.2.4, as translated by Max Muller.
48. Michael Allen, "The Hindu View of Women," in *Women in India and Nepal*, p. 17.
49. Ibid., p. 19.
50. Ibid., p. 5.
51. Ibid., p. 9.
52. Ibid., p. 11.
53. See, for example, Manikkavachakar's *Tiruvachakam*, translated by Ratna Navaratnam. Bombay: Bharatiya Vidya Bhavan, 1975.
54. See *Yogadarśanam of Patañjali*. Varanasi: Bhāratīya Vidyā Prakāśana, 1963, II.5. English translations consulted include: J. H. Woods, *The Yoga System of Patañjali*. Delhi: Motilal Banarsidass, 1966; Rama Prasada, *Yoga Sūtras of Patañjali*. Delhi: Oriental Books Reprint Corporation, 1978, and Bangali Baba, *The Yoga Sūtra of Patañjali*. Delhi: Motilal Banarsidass, 1976.
55. From Vyāsa's "Commentary" on *Yoga Sūtra* II.5, as translated by J. H. Woods.
56. From Vacaspati Miśra's "Explanation" on *Yoga Sūtra* II.5, as translated by J. H. Woods.
57. See Sāṇkhya theory as formulated, around the same time, in the *Sāṅkhya Kārikā of Īśvara Krishna*, trans. By J. Davies. Calcutta: Susil Gupta, 1947.
58. *Yoga Sūtra*, II.18, Commentary (*bhāṣya*).
59. See Gopinath Kaviraj, "The Doctrine of Pratibhā in Indian Philosophy," *Annals of the Bhandarkar Oriental Research Institute*, 1924, pp. 1–18 and 113–132.
60. *Yoga Sūtra*, II.18, Commentary (*bhāṣya*).
61. *Yoga Sūtras*, II.12–14 & IV.7–9. The following is a summary of *karma* as found in these passages of the *Yoga Sūtras:*

Karma has its origin in afflictions	— *kleśamūlah karmāśavah* (Sūtra II. 12)
It ripens into life-states, life-experiences, and life-time, if the root exists	— *sati mūle takvipāko jātyāyyurbhogāh* (Sūtra II. 13)
Those [life-states, etc.], as the fruit, are pleasant or unpleasant, because they are produced from virtuous or non-virtuous causes.	— *te hlādaparitāpaphalāh punyāpunyahetuvāt* (Sūtra II. 14)

To those who understand, all [of those] is indeed pain, because change, anxiety, and habituation are painful and [the life-states, etc.] obstruct the operations of virtuous qualities.	— *parināmatapasamskāraduhkhair gunavrttivirodhāc ca duhkham eva sarvam vivekinah* (Sūtra II. 15)

In *Yoga Sūtra, karma* is equal to *vāsanā*

A Yogin's *karma* is niether white nor black: for [all] others, it is threefold.	— *karmāsuklākrsnam yoginas trividham itareṣām* (Sūtra IV. 7)
From the [threefold karma] there come the impressions (*vāsanā*) of only those which are capable of bringing about their fruition.	— *tatas tadvipākānugunānām ekābhivyaktir vāsanānām* (Sūtra IV. 8)

In *Yoga Sūtra, smṛti* is equal to *saṁskāra*

[The process of impression] continues uninterruptedly, even though there is a time lapse between births, places, and time, because memory and memory traces are of one substance. (Note: here, *saṁskāra* is better translated 'memory traces', because unlike Sutra II. 15, *saṁskāra* is equated to *smṛti*.)	— *jātidesakālavyavahitānām apy ānantaryam smrtisamskārayor ekarūpatvāt* (Sūtra IV. 9) *Commentary states: kutaś ca smrtisamskāravor ekarūpatvāt/yathānubhavās tathā amskārāh te ca karmavāsanārūpāh/yathā ca vāsanās tahtā smrtir iti/jātidesakālavyavahitebhyah samskārebhyah smṛtiḥ smṛtiś ca punah samskārā ity evam ete smrtisaṁskārāh karmāśayavrttilābhavaṡāveṡād abhivayajyante / . . . . /vāsanāh samskārā āsayā ity arthah/*

Therefore, according to this:

smṛti—samskāra—smṛti: the continuation of which is supported by *karma* (*karmābhivyañjakam*) and *vāsanā* functions as the support for *samskāra* (memory traces) which produce *smṛti* (memory).

62. From "Commentary" on *Yoga Sūtra* II.1 as translated by Rama Prasada, p. 88.
63. Information on tradition from Prof. T. R. V. Murti, Banaras Hindu University, July 1972.
64. See *The Hathayogapradīpikā of Svātmārāma* with English translation. Adyar: Adyar Library and Research Centre, 1972. The practice of *dhauti* or swallowing a wet piece of cloth is described in II.24.
65. *Yoga Sūtra* II.40, translation by J. H. Woods.
66. *Yoga Sūtra* II.40, Commentary of Vyāsa, translated by J. H. Woods, p. 188.
67. *The Bhagavad-Gītā*, translated by R. C. Zaehner. Oxford: Oxford University Press, 1969, I.42, p. 119.
68. *Yoga Sūtra* II.43, Commentary of Vyāsa, translated by J. H. Woods, p. 189.

69. *Yoga Sūtra* I.16, Explanation of Vacaspati Miśra trans. by Rama Prasada, p. 31.

70. *Yoga Sūtra* I.41.

71. *Yoga Sūtra* I.47–51.

72. The above information on Gorakhnāth is taken from George Weston Briggs, *Gorakhnāth and the Kānphaṭa Yogīs*. Delhi: Motilal Banarsidass, 1973, pp. 228–249.

73. Ibid., Cp. 12.

74. The ten chief *nādis* are *idā, piṅglā, susumṇā, gāndhārī, hastijihvā, pūṣā, yaśasvinī, alambuṣā, būhūś* and *śaṁkhinī*. They terminate respectively in the left nostril, the right nostril, the hole-in-the skull (anterior fontanell), the left eye, the right eye, the right ear, the left ear, the mouth, the male organ and the anus. See *Gorakhnāth and the Kānphaṭa Yogīs*, Cp 15, for more details.

75. As quoted by Briggs from *Haṭhayogapradīpika* I.58., p. 309.

76. The above practices are described in Chapter Two of the *Haṭhayogapradīpika*.

77. For details see Chapters Two and Three of the *Haṭhyogapradīpika*.

78. See Chapter Four of the *Haṭhyogapradīpika* and "The Gorakṣa Śataḳa" of Gorakhnāth, verse 101, as translated by G. W. Briggs in *Gorakhnāth and the Kānphaṭa Yogīs*, p. 304.

79. *The Gorakṣa Śataḳa*, translation by G. W. Briggs, *Gorakhnāth and the Kānphaṭa Yogis*, p. 304. See also verse 82, p. 303.

80. *Gorakṣa Śataḳa*, verse 905, Briggs p. 303.

81. *Gorakṣa Śataḳa*, verse 58, Briggs p. 296.

82. *Gorakṣa Śataḳa*, verse 73, Briggs, p. 299.

83. Shashibhusan Dasgupta, *Obscure Religious Cults*. Calcutta: Firma K. L. Mukhopadhyay, 1962, p. 249.

84. Ibid., p. 223.

85. Ibid., p. 244.

86. Ibid., p. 245.

87. Ibid., p. 99.

88. Ibid., p. 153.

89. Wendy Doniger O'Flaherty, *Women, Androgynes and Other Mythical Beasts*, Chicago: University of Chicago Press, 1982, p. 40.

90. Ibid., p. 42.

91. Ibid., p. 60.

92. Dasgupta, *Obscure Religious Cults*, p. 393.

93. See Dasgupta, "Mayanāmatī, "Appendix C of *Obscure Religious Cults*, pp. 397–398.

94. Alexander Lipski, *The Life and Teaching of Srī Ānandamayī Mā*, Delhi: Motilal Banarsidass, 1977, pp. 6–7.

95. Briggs, *Gorakhnāth and the Kānphaṭa Yogis*, p. 27.

96. Ibid., p. 34.

97. Basham, *The Wonder That Was India*, p. 178. Basham adds that, in general in medieval India, women were not encouraged to take up a life of religion or asceticism. "Their true function was marriage and the care of their menfolk and children." p. 178.

98. Swami Iśwarananda, *Does the Soul Reincarnate?* Trichur: Sri Ramakrishna Ashrama, 1964, pp. 44, 50–51.

99. Sanat Kumar Sen, "Indian Philosophy and Social Ethics," *Journal of the Indian Academy of Philosophy*, vol. 6, 1967, pp. 67–68.

100. See S. Gopalan, "Karma, Rebirth and the Hindu Philosophy of the Individual and Society," *Indian Philosophical Annual*, vol. 1, 1965, pp. 153–154. See also Paramanheri Sundaram Sivaswamy Aiyer, *Evolution of Hindu Moral Ideals*. Calcutta: Calcutta University, 1935, p. 149j.

101. Swami Vivekananda, *Collected Works*, VIII., pp. 262–263.

102. Sarasvati Chennakesavan, *Concepts of Indian Philosophy*. Columbia, Mo.: South Asia Books, 1976, p. 223.

103. *The Constitution of India* proclaimed by the Indian Constituent Assembly, Nov. 26, 1949, p. 1.

104. Donald Eugene Smith, *India as a Secular State*. Princeton: Princeton University Press, 1963, p. 108.

105. Ibid.

106. The case referred to is that of *Taher Saifuddin v. Tyebbhai Moosaji* cited by Smith, p. 110. See also Robert Baird, "Religion and the Secular: Categories for Religious Conflict and Religious Change in Independent India," *Journal of Asian and African Studies*, vol. XI, 1987, pp. 47–63.

107. See, for example, the Supreme Court Case *Sri Venkataramana Devaru v. State of Mysore*, Nov. 1957, Appeal No. 327.

2. *The Classical Hindu View on Abortion and the Moral Status of the Unborn**

JULIUS J. LIPNER

I. Clarification of Terms

LET US start with a few clarifications, the better to focus our perspective and concerns. At present, the nature and moral status of the human unborn, considered in various contexts (genetic research, in vitro fertilisation, abortion, surrogate motherhood, and so on), form a topic of intense discussion in the West. In India, however, these issues, for the most part, still lie below the surface in the public mind, or, to change the metaphor, have yet to come out of the closet.[1] It is all the more important, therefore, to broach this topic in preparation for the Indian debate that needs must arise, especially from the Hindu viewpoint—the viewpoint of the majority of Indians. In the process, I hope some light will be shed on the complexities of the Western discussion. The approach in this essay has primarily the moral angle in view, though it will also be necessary, where relevant, to make philosophical, historical, medical, and other observations. Further, in the Hindu context, this vast area of study is, for the most part, uncharted in any systematic way. For this reason, we shall focus on the concept of abortion as being the most suitable handle to come to grips with the complex web of ideas which makes up the Hindu view of the moral status of the unborn. Indeed, it will bring us to the heart of the matter.

---

*This essay is dedicated to Fr. George Gispert-Sauch, S.J., of Vidyajyoti, Institute of Religious Studies, Delhi—sound scholar and good friend.

In this chapter, abortion is to be understood in the causative sense, that is, as the deliberate effecting of a miscarriage, a deliberate termination of pregnancy. Abortion, then, is to be distinguished from involuntary miscarriage. As we shall see, this is an important distinction, not least in the Sanskritic tradition, and it is not always observed in discussions like this, especially when translations of the relevant Sanskrit terms are involved. For the purposes of this essay, one limit of our study will be the moment prior to (human) conception; the other limit will be the birth of the infant. Thus, we shall not consider issues relating to contraception, and so on, on the one hand, or stillbirth, infanticide, etc. on the other.

Moreover, we shall be concerned with the CLASSICAL Hindu view. In effect, our study will rely on Sanskrit texts ranging from about 600 B.C.E. to 600 C.E. These texts will be taken from both *śruti* and *smṛti;* the former term denotes the canonical scriptures of the Hindus, comprising the Vedas and including the Upaniṣads, while the latter term refers to the numerous non-canonical scriptures whose authority derives from their alleged corroboration and illumination of *śruti*. In point of fact, under *smṛti* we shall refer mainly to the seminal writings on law (*Dharmasūtras* and *Dharmaśāstras*), to some *Purāṇas* (repositories of folklore and popular religion), to that great epic, the *Mahābhārata* (a compendium similar to the *Purāṇas*), and to the medical works of Caraka and Suśruta—all of which found their present form in the period mentioned. No doubt to contextualize the classical view so demarcated, we shall have to take note of Hindu thinking before and after this period, but there can be no doubt that it was from about 600 B.C.E. to 600 C.E. that the definitive Hindu view on the moral status of the unborn in connection with abortion was developed and established. This is a view which, in its essentials, remained unchanged through succeeding centuries and which continues to exert a powerful influence on the contemporary Hindu mind. It is in this sense only that I use "classical" to describe the context of our study.

Here we may note the distinction implied in the Sanskrit between the terms for abortion (*garbha-*, *bhrūṇa-: hatyā, vadha*) and those for (involuntary) miscarriage. The former terms assume that a morally reprehensible killing (*hatyā*) has taken place, rather than an ethically neutral evacuation, dislodging, or excision, for example, while, as we are about to see, the standard Sanskrit words for miscarriage refer simply to a falling or emission (of the embryo[2]). The law books and law manuals (*Dharmasūtras* and *Dharmaśāstras*),[3] as well as the medical texts, are standard sources for the various terms for miscarriage. Chiefly to correspond to different forms of ritual purification for the mother and her kinsfolk, various "descent" words are applied in Sanskrit to miscarriage as it occurs during different stages in pregnancy. The lawbook of Gautama (*Gautamadharmasūtra: GauDS*), a work of about 6th century B.C.E.,[4] under II.5.15, speaks of miscarriage as a *sraṃsana* (a falling or dropping).[5] A later authority, the well-known law manual, the *Manusmṛti* (*MnS*), 200 B.C.E.–200 C.E.,[6] uses *garbhasrāva* (the flow or issue of the embryo) to refer to the same event.[7] The authoritative *Yājñavalkyasmṛti* (*YjS*), 1st.–3d. century of the Christian era[8] also refers to *garbhasrāva*, under III.20: "In the case of miscarriage (*garbhasrāva*) (observance of the purification ritual for) as many nights as correspond to the months (of pregnancy) causes purity."[9] Commenting on this text, Vijñāneśvara, in his *Mitākṣarā* (*Mit.*) 11th.–12th. century, the most authoritative and well-known commentary on the *YjS*, makes reference to miscarriage occurring at different periods in pregnancy by way of specific "descent" terms. Quoting Marīci, an accepted authority on *dharma* (the law as supportive of right living, from *dhṛ*, to support), the *Mit.* says: "Till the fourth (month of pregnancy, miscarriage) would be an 'emission' (*srāva*), and a 'fall' (*pāta*) for the fifth and sixth (months); after that it would be an 'issue' (*prasūti*), while in the tenth month it would be a 'generation' (*sūtaka*, i.e., tantamount to a stillbirth?)."[10] In all these instances, the distinction is preserved, in terminology as well as in intention, between what we have described as abortion and as miscarriage.[11] This becomes luminously clear from the way the texts morally evaluate these two events.

II. Abortion: Moral Evaluation in *Śruti*

We may begin by simply pointing out that the earliest *śruti* texts attest that the embryo in the womb is specially deserving of protection and that, indeed, abortion is a morally intolerable act. In the *Ṛg Saṃhitā* (which embodies some of the earliest recorded canonical scriptures of the Hindus, dating possibly to before 1200 B.C.E.) the deity Viṣṇu is referred to as "protector of the child-to-be."[12] The implication here is clearly that the embryo requires special protection because of its moral inviolability and physical vulnerability; this protection is sought from Viṣṇu who, from Vedic times to the present, has always been regarded as the special preserver of life and order.[13] The *Atharva Veda* (equally old, possibly older in parts) expresses the same attitude towards the unborn child, with the added implication that abortion counts amongst the most heinous crimes. In VI.113.2 (see also VI.112.3) we have: "Enter thou into the rays, into smoke, O sin. Begone into the vapours and into the mists! Be lost in the foam of the rivers. While thou, O Pūṣan, wipe off (our) misdeeds on the slayer of the embryo (*bhrūṇaghni*)."[14] Such a "wiping off" is always recommended upon the worst offenders.[15] The *Śatapatha Brāhmaṇa* (which belongs to a period after that of the Vedic hymns) invokes what is obviously the general view on human abortion when it condemns those who consume beef: "Such people have a bad reputation, of the kind 'He's extracted the embryo from a mother,' 'He's an evildoer.'"[16]

There are clearer indications of disapproval by the time we come to the Upaniṣads (most of which fall within the classical period). Thus the *Bṛhadāraṇyaka Upaniṣad* (one of the oldest Upaniṣads, probably 8th–9th century B.C.E.), when describing a form of mystical experience, notes: "Here the father is no longer a father, the mother no longer a mother, the (post-mortem) worlds are no longer such worlds, the gods no longer gods, the Vedas no longer Vedas. The thief is no longer a thief, the slayer of the embryo (*bhrūṇahā*) no longer a slayer of the embryo, the Cāṇḍāla and the Paulkasa are no longer such,[17] nor are the monk and the ascetic. Both merit and demerit cease to have effect, for then one has crossed over every concern of the heart."[18] The Upaniṣad is referring to a state of awareness in which the most significant worldly relationships and designations for the Hindu cease to have meaning. What concerns us is the place accorded to the slayer of the embryo (*bhrūṇahā*) here. Such a person, in contrast to the most idealised members of society (the monk and the ascetic), is relegated to a position among the vilest, viz., the thief (especially the culprit who steals from a Brahmin) and the most contaminating outcasts. In other words, abortion violated *dharma*—the socio-religious order—in a most serious way. This implies that the living embryo enjoyed a special moral status in the eyes of the Hindu and was specially deserving of protection and respect. The reasons for this we shall inquire into later.

We may conclude this brief review of the *śruti* position on abortion by quoting from one or two later Upaniṣads. In commending intimate knowledge of the deity, Indra, in III.1 the *Kauṣītaki Upaniṣad* says in his name: "For him who knows me, his (post-mortem) world is not lost on account of any action—not by stealing, nor by abortion, nor by killing one's mother or father. . . ."[19] Here the text implicitly stresses that abortion (*bhrūṇahatyā* is the term used) is a reprehensible killing, for it is ranked alongside particularly heinous forms of murder. For its part, the *Mahānārāyaṇa Upaniṣad* lists the abortionist with such offenders as the violator of the guru's bed (*gurutalpaga*), the one who is unfaithful to his vow of chastity (*avakīrṇī*), and the drunkard (*surāpāna*).[20]

III. Abortion: Moral Evaluation in *Smṛti*

We turn now to the occasionally more explicit *smṛti* texts, in order to give a clearer picture of the recommended view of the status of the unborn (and of the censure attaching to abortion). We can accomplish this end in two ways: (a) by showing that the texts concur in fostering special respect and making special allowances for the pregnant woman, and (b) by noting the explicit condemnation of (and punishment for) abortion in these sources.

(A) Attitude to Pregnant Women

The so-called *Viṣṇudharmasūtra* (*ViDS*) or *Law Book of Viṣṇu* (the relevant prose sections of which Kane ascribes to 300 B.C.E. to 100 C.E.[21]) protects the pregnant woman (and indeed the embryo directly) by equating the killing of either with one of the most serious offences a Hindu could commit, viz. the killing of a Brahmin. In *ViDS* XXXVI.1 we read: "Killing a Kṣatriya or a Vaiśya engaged in sacrifice, a menstruating woman, a pregnant woman . . . (and) . . . the embryo (even) of a stranger . . . is tantamount to killing a Brahmin."[22] Elsewhere, we read that the penance for killing a pregnant woman unintentionally is the same as that for unintentionally killing a Brahmin (L.6–8), though, perhaps surprisingly, only the penance for unintentionally killing a king is greater.

Other forms of protection/respect for the pregnant woman are in evidence. In the same law text, it is laid down that "the ferry-man or toll-official who collects from a student (engaged in sacred study), a forest-dweller (who has renounced worldly life), a (religious) mendicant, a pregnant woman, and one on pilgrimage (is to be fined)."[23] The *Mahābhārata* (*Mbh.*, 400 B.C.E.–400 C.E.) has it that: "One must give way to the Brahmin, to cows, to kings, to the old, to one burdened by a load, to a pregnant woman and to the infirm."[24] More tellingly, under *YjS* I.86, the *Mit.* recommends con-cremation (*anvārohaṇa*, i.e., *suttee*) as the righteous action for all wives except those who are pregnant or have young children to care for,[25] while there is a charming suggestion in Caraka that the pregnant woman in her delicate condition should be treated like a vessel brimful of oil: she should not be agitated lest a mishap occur.[26] From these examples, the idea emerges that, for the Hindus, pregnancy was a very special state and that the unborn had a (moral) status meriting protection. This conclusion is substantiated by noting what the texts have to say in condemning abortion.

(B) Condemnation of Abortion

Here there can be no doubt about the reprehensibility of abortion. The censure applying to this deed is severe indeed. In the *GauDS* (III.3.9), we are told that a woman loses caste by committing abortion and by sexual connection with men of lower castes.[27] The *Law Book of Āpastamba* (*Āpastambadharmasūtra: ApDS*), to which Kane assigns a date probably a century or two later than the *GauDS*,[28] makes the same point: "Now these (are the actions which) lead to a fall from caste: stealing . . . murder . . . abortion, sexual union with women with whom one is related maternally or paternally. . . ."[29] Now, loss of caste was a terrible consequence for a Hindu to face, especially in traditional times. Acceptance of and in caste determined one's way of life, one's social viability, and even one's prospects for salvation. Further, this had far-reaching consequences for the socio-religious standing of one's family. Loss of caste, then, was one of the ultimate socio-religious penalties of Hindu *dharma* (though it was not necessarily irrevocable).

Other forms of punishment for abortion are found in the law texts. Manu forbids ancestral liberations of water (*udakakriyā*) to be offered "to women who were reprobates, sexually promiscuous, who harmed the embryo or its mother, and who took to liquor."[30] The *YjS* prescribes a considerable fine[31] to "the destroyer of the embryo of a female slave" (*dāsīgarbhavināśakṛt*), while under II.277 it lays down that "the highest punishment is due for injury with a weapon and for abortion."[32] As the *Mit.* makes clear, in the latter case it is abortions other than those pertaining to female slaves and Brahmin women (*dāsībrāhmaṇagarbhavyatirekena*) which are referred to, these two cases being covered by separate injunctions.[33] Hindu lawgivers legislated according to circumstances. The embryo of a caste Hindu (especially of a Brahmin) was more deserving of protection than the embryo of a slave, analogous to the way the life of a virtuous person was deemed more valuable, for one reason or another, than the life of a rogue.[34] But the fact that, even in the case of the slave, abortion was regarded as punishable, indeed the very discrepancy between punishments for "high" and "low" abortions, is an indication that in classical times abortion, at least without the gravest reasons as we shall see, was morally unacceptable.

Evidence of the Mahābhārata

Here we may look at the evidence of the *Mbh.* against the acceptability of abortion. The *Mbh.* may be regarded as representative of authoritative classical texts on *dharma* which retain, for our purposes, relevant, popular appeal. We can point to at least four contexts in the *Mbh.* in which abortion is condemned.

1. Abortion is regarded as an instance of extreme transgression the better to emphasise the seriousness of other crimes. In *Mbh.* XII.86.26, to stress the king's obligation to give safe conduct to an envoy or ambassador of the enemy, it is said: "If a king is intent upon the code of the (battle-)field but slays an envoy who speaks as he has been commanded—his ancestors incur (the crime of) abortion."[35]
2. Abortion is referred to to indicate the great importance in which legitimate procreation was held in the society of the day (towards

the chief end of begetting a son, for weighty economic, social, and religious reasons). The first book of the *Mbh.* has it that, "He who does not accede, when importuned privately, to a willing and available woman, is called a killer of the embryo by those wise in matters of law."[36] This passage seems to invoke the early tradition of *niyoga* or levirate as it obtained in Hindu society.

3. Reference is made to abortion so as to exalt the religious importance of the *Mbh.* "There can be no doubt that the wise man, having heard this Veda of Kṛṣṇa (Dvaipāyana, i.e., the *Mbh.*) would shed even the crime of abortion."[37]
4. Reference to abortion is used as a device to exalt the Brahmin. Bhīṣma advises Yudhiṣṭhira: "O excellent one, the twice-born (i.e., Brahmins) must be protected. Even if they are grave offenders you should only banish them from your dominions (-harm them no further). Chief of all, you should show mercy to the transgressors among them, even for slaying a Brahmin, violating the guru's bed, or killing an embryo."[38]

From these contexts, it is clear that abortion was reckoned a serious wrong.

Here we may consider a possible counter-example from the *Mbh.* in which abortion seems to be countenanced. In fact, in the context of this essay, it will be instructive to analyse this example. The story goes that the powerful sage Vyāsa once granted Gāndhārī (the wife of the king Dhṛtarāṣṭra) a boon. Gāndhārī chose to have a hundred sons. In due course, she was made pregnant by the king and remained in this state for two years. Eventually, and in despair no doubt, "Gāndhārī—unbeknown to Dhṛtarāṣṭra—aborted her womb with great effort, fainting with grief. A fleshy lump came out, compact as a ball of iron"[39] which Gāndhārī sought to dispose of. Vyāsa had seen it all by his yogic perception and literally flew to the rescue (superman!) to thwart the natural consequences of Gāndhārī's act. First, however, he upbraids her ("What's this you've wanted to do!": *kim idaṃ te cikīrṣitam*), then he commands that a hundred pots (*kuṇḍa*—not unlike the womb in shape) be quickly filled with *ghee* (clarified butter) and that the ball of flesh be sprinkled with cool water. The narrative continues: "That doused ball then separated into a hundred parts, each an embryo no larger than a thumb-joint in size."[40] Each embryo was then deposited in one of the pots, and the pots were stored in a safe place. Having instructed Gāndhārī as to when the pots were to be broken for the "delivery" of the children, Vyāsa departed to continue his austerities. In time, Gāndhārī got her hundred sons (by what seems to be an early substitute for in vitro gestation . . !).

Now the point is that abortion is not really being condoned in the story. To begin with, Gāndhārī aborts "fainting with grief"; in spite of her desperation, she is aware that she is transgressing the ethical code by her deed. In fact, this is why Vyāsa rebukes her when he arrives on the scene. A chief purpose of the story is to show that an ascetic's word can never be void, however impossible of materialisation it might appear (and Vyāsa was an exceptional ascetic). Vyāsa had promised Gāndhārī a hundred sons, and a hundred sons she would have. Recourse to the abortion, hedged as the act is with disclaimers and qualifications, is the literary device required for the realisation of Vyāsa's promise. In the event, the abortion does not have its natural consequence but is redeemed by Vyāsa's prescribing a surrogate gestation. All's well in the end. The *Mbh.* (and *Purāṇas* for that matter) abound with stories in which apparent abortions/miscarriages actually do come to term by some means or other. In the end, the sanctity of the embryo is upheld.

IV. Abortion: A Moral As Well As A Social Concern

At this point, an objection may be raised to the general thesis so far: For the Hindus, abortion may well have been a social rather than a moral transgression. Do the texts not imply that it is abortion among (licitly impregnated) caste-Hindus, rather than among outsiders, that is being censured? So was abortion not reprehensible because it imperiled the stability and preservation of the Hindu social order, rather than because it primarily violated the worth of the human individual? By implication, the unborn would not enjoy then a primarily MORALLY inviolable status, but a primarily SOCIALLY inviolable one.

Anyone who makes this objection has not grasped the nature of traditional Hindu *dharma*—that which upholds right precept and practice—for which social and moral values were inextricably intertwined. No doubt the immediate concern of the Hindu lawgivers and law enforcers was the values of established Hindu society as they obtained for the members of that society. And no doubt in this context abortion was seen to have unacceptable social consequences. We have seen that this was the case. But there was a strong moral element in the Hindu condemnation of abortion, with the implication that the perception of the status of the unborn had no less a moral than a social dimension. This has already been indicated in the course of this essay, but it is as well to clarify the issue.

We start by noting that in the various lists given above, abortion is placed among transgressions which not only have undesirable social consequences but which also attract strong moral condemnation. Thus though abortion is listed with drunkenness, incest, and illicit miscegenation of the castes (which, it MIGHT be argued, are predominantly social transgressions), it is also listed with unchastity (recognised to have a private, and therefore overtly moral, dimension), thieving, violating one's guru's bed, and, especially, killing: killing one's father or mother, and killing, in general (*puruṣavadha*).[41] Abortion even vis-à-vis the female slave is condemned, notwithstanding the fact that female slaves and servants were not exalted members of Hindu society.[42] Further, the *Mit.* forbids *suttee*, an act with strong social overtones, to pregnant wives, implying thereby that the unborn have a (moral) status which must not be subjected to social demands. One cannot argue here that a stronger social need (producing children, especially sons) takes precedence over a weaker social need (*suttee*). The *Mit.* does not say that pregnant women who already have the desired number or kind (i.e., males) of children may ascend the funeral pyre. In fact, the contrary is implied.[43] In connection with all this, we must remember that Sanskrit usage clearly distinguishes between two kinds of event: involuntary termination of pregnancy (miscarriage), and deliberate termination of pregnancy (abortion). In contrast to words for miscarriage, abortion terms are always positive killing terms (*-hatyā*). In context, it is difficult to see how such usage could not have had a significant moral connotation. The fact that the texts were immediately directed at caste-Hindus does not mean that they lacked a more universal moral perspective. Morally and socially, it was generally assumed that the Hindu way was the superior way. Thus the distinctively moral Hindu ideals and judgments tacitly applied to one and all. From this we conclude that the unborn, in classical Hindu tradition, were accorded a moral status deserving of special protection and that abortion was generally reprehensible because thereby the integrity of the human person (of both victim and abortionist) was seriously violated.

We can throw into relief what has been said thus far by considering now a situation in which abortion was permitted by an authoritative classical text. This is the *Suśruta Saṃhitā*, a seminal medical treatise of uncertain date (in its present form probably of 3d–4th century C.E., though reference is made to an original, which may have been in existence two or three centuries before the Christian Era). In the "Cikitsāsthāna" chapter of this work, in the section called "The Foetus Astray" (*mūḍhgarbha*), the eventuality of aborting the foetus is considered.

The text begins by pointing out that "there is nothing as difficult as the delivery of a foetus astray in the womb, for here . . . the job must be done 'by feel' . . . by one hand, without injury to mother or foetus (if possible)."[44] The text continues: "If the foetus is alive, one should attempt to remove it from the womb of the mother (alive)."[45] No doubt is left as to the ideal to be striven for: the safety of both mother and child. However, if the foetus is dead (*mṛte garbhe*), it may be removed by cutting (and dismembering, if necessary; *sūtra* 9). The text then considers the situation in which the live foetus cannot be safely delivered. In this event, it forbids removal by surgery. "For if (the foetus) be cut one would harm both mother and her offspring. In an irredeemable situation, it is best to cause the miscarriage of the foetus, for no means must be neglected which can prevent the loss of the mother."[46] Abortion then[47] is the last recourse, only when it is clearly a question of weighing life against life—the life of the mother against that of the foetus. Throughout, the lives of both are accorded the greatest respect. It is highly unlikely that the text here was departing from generally held views in the matter. To say that its judgement was without primary moral content would be absurd.

We may adduce one more consideration to show that, in classical times, the question of abortion and of the status of the unborn was invested with at least as much moral as social significance. Indeed, as we shall see, moral considerations seem to hold their own in what was importantly a social issue. This issue concerns the strong aversion, in the ethical codes, to "reprehensible" procreation, especially reprehensible procreation between members of different castes and the procreation between caste-Hindus and outcastes. Such reprehensible intercaste procreation in general was called *varṇasaṃkara* (mixing of the castes). In our discussion, we shall refer to it as "miscegenation".

In traditional Hindu society three kinds of issue resulting from sexual union were recognised: 1. the offspring of "marriage proper," that is, of licit marriages between members of the same caste; 2. the product of permissible or *anuloma* intercaste marriages (i.e., marriages "in accordance with the sweep of the hair"). For such unions, the man had to belong to the higher caste; and 3. the issue of reprehensible unions, i.e., of (a) either illicit sex between people of the same or of *anuloma* status, or (b) what were called *pratiloma* unions (viz., intercourse "against the sweep of the hair"). In *pratiloma* unions, the woman belonged to the higher caste; the greater the caste disparity between the partners, the more reprehensible both union and offspring. We are especially concerned with the children of reprehensible intercaste procreation or miscegenation. Such children were generally at a great disadvantage in society, most of them being regarded as ritually impure or untouchable. Among the most despised of such offspring were the Cāṇḍāla (the child of a Brahmin mother and a Śūdra father) and the Paulkasa (usually the child of a Kṣatriya mother and a Śūdra father).[48] The situation was complicated greatly by the fact that the offspring of *pratiloma* unions could themselves miscegenate, often thus producing new categories of outcastes.

The aversion in which miscegenation, in general, was held in traditional Hindu society is evident from the popular texts. The *Bhagavad-Gītā* provides a good example. In the very first chapter, the warrior Arjuna is recounting to his friend the Lord, Kṛṣṇa, the evil consequences of war: the social relationships between the various clans become gravely upset.

> When the clan is destroyed, the enduring clan-rules collapse. When Rule collapses, disorder overtakes the whole clan. From the ascendancy of disorder, Kṛṣṇa, the clan-women are vitiated. When the women are vitiated, then miscegenation occurs. Miscegenation results in hell for the destroyers of the clan and for the clan itself—for the ancestral fathers of such fall (from their heavens), their (post-mortem) libations and offerings having lapsed. By these crimes of the clan-destroyers—that is, bringing about miscegenation—the eternal laws of the clan and of the race are abolished. Once the eternal clan-rules of the people are abolished, Kṛṣṇa, one resides in hell eternal—thus have we heard.[49]

This is grave indictment indeed.

Pratiloma persons, therefore, especially the most despised groups, were subjected in the society of the time to what, by any standards, were intolerable socio-religious strictures. Yet nowhere in texts, so far as I know, is it formally recommended that abortion be resorted to as an acceptable way out, either to avert an insufferable life for the *pratiloma* child-to-be or to safeguard the parents from ignominy. On the contrary, elaborate provision was made in the law texts concerning the avocations and rules of life of *pratiloma* persons.[50] Clearly their right to life in the face of adverse social consequences both for themselves and for their parents was recognised and safeguarded.[51]

V. Reasons for the Classical View

Now, in this part of the essay, let us inquire into the main reasons for this view on abortion and the moral status of the unborn in classical times.

A Philosophical Distinction

It will be helpful to start the discussion by reference to a distinction often made by some contemporary western moralists in the context of the moral status of the embryo/foetus. In this context, these moralists affirm that a distinction is in order between the individual qua HUMAN BEING and the individual qua HUMAN PERSON. The individual qua human being, they say, is a member of the human species but, for various reasons, is not yet a person—in fact, may never be a person. Some of these limiting reasons may be the following: the lack of a recognisable human form (in the embryo/foetus); clear evidence (detected by mechanical devices) of insufficient (rather than abnormal) cerebral activity in some foetuses compared to cerebral activity, in other foetuses, which is accepted and established as pertaining to human persons at that stage of development, and so on. The moralists differ as to whether one or more of such reasons are the sufficient condition to determine human personhood.

It is not to the point here to inquire whether the criteria themselves and the distinction based on them, are valid. The point is that some moralists, having established to their satisfaction criteria for distinguishing between human beings and human persons (or at least, for the validity of this distinction), then go on to affirm that abortion in the case of human BEINGS is morally permissible for reasons which may not be valid when abortion of human PERSONS is in question. In practical terms, they incline to the view that abortion in the early stages of pregnancy cannot be objected to morally with the same force as to abortion in the late stages of pregnancy ("early" and "late" here are given varying interpretations). This is because in early pregnancy, the human being has not yet developed—for one reason or another—into the human person with the latter's claim to a moral status qualitatively superior to that of the former (however "human person" may then be further defined).

Now, we may ask, is the classical Hindu view on the nature of the prenatal human individual such as to permit us to draw this kind of qualitative distinction between human being and human person, with its repercussions for the (limited) permissibility of abortion? To answer this, we shall have to examine first the traditional Hindu philosophical position on the nature of human personhood.

The Hindu View of Personhood

It is well known that there are many views in Hindu tradition during our period on the nature of the human person. Nevertheless, in this respect, one and only one basic model—with variations on the theme—was accepted from early times in traditional, orthodox Hinduism (viz., in those perspectives or *darśanas* which did not explicitly repudiate the authority of the accredited scriptures). According to this basic model, the human person is a composite of two essentially disparate but intimately conjoined principles—spirit (*ātman, puruṣa*) and matter (*prakṛti*). Spirit is essentially the locus of consciousness and bliss, and is impervious to substantial change; matter is essentially insentient, tending to diversification and change. For reasons we need not go into here, spirit and matter come together to produce the distinctive individual which each of us is. This union, though finally dissoluble, is nevertheless a profound one and engenders the separate centres of self-awareness we experience ourselves to be. This experience is characterised by the congenital illusion which fails to distinguish between the "real" self, that is, the pure spirit, and the "false" or composite self (matter-cum-spirit). Liberation, the human goal, about which the different schools have different views, necessarily consists in at least the internalised awareness of the distinction between the real self and the false self. So long as this enlightened knowledge is not attained, each of us repeatedly dies and is physically reborn as a continuum of different personalities, each reborn individual being determined as to nature and life situation by the resultant of the continuum's past ego-centred KARMA (i.e., meritorious and unmeritorious action). This process of *karma* and rebirth is beginningless for each individual and may continue indefinitely. It is terminated by enlightenment, and at death the enlightened soul is liberated from the wheel of rebirth.

This basic model of human personhood is delineated in the *Caraka Saṃhitā*.[52] The quotations that follow are taken from a philosophical section of this treatise called the *Śārīrasthāna*. It was typical of the integral outlook of the Hindu mind that a medical text also contained discussions on the nature of the human subject. The Hindus believed that a physician could not effectively minister to the body unless he viewed it in the perspective of the spirit.

In the section mentioned, the following description of the spirit or *ātman's* essential nature is given as the evidently acceptable one: "Those who know the *ātman* say that it is actionless, self-dependent, sovereign, all-pervading, and omnipresent; that it has conscious control over the body (that is, is a *kṣetrajña*) and witnesses its doings."[53] Later the inner self (*antarātman*) of the human person is described as essentially "eternal, free from disease, free from old age, deathless, free from decay; it cannot be pierced, cut or agitated. It takes all forms, performs all actions, is unmanifest, beginningless, endless and immutable."[54] In answer to how it is then that, in the human subject, the *ātman* (as described above) seems to manifest the contrary characteristics, viz., being a limited agent, mortal, dependent upon bodily functions, changeable, and so on, we are told that this false appearance of the *ātman* results from the *ātman's* union with matter (in the form of the body). The body, for its part, is described as, "the support of the conscious principle, constitutive of the totality of modifications of the five elementals (which make up matter), and maintaining the harmonious conjunction (of its parts)."[55]

Ensoulment, and Consciousness in the Womb

With this traditional Hindu view of human personhood in mind, let us consider now, in the context of the distinction between human being and human person and its implications for abortion, what the classical texts have to say about the nature of human conception and the development of the embryo. Here we seem to be confronted with two traditions—what we may call a "major" (because of its apparently weightier authority) and a "minor" (which, in contrast to the major, seems to rely on weaker evidence).

Focusing on the major tradition first, there follows a description of what happens at conception, taken from the section entitled "Descent (of the spirit) into the womb" of the *Caraka Saṃhitā:* "Conception occurs when intercourse takes place in due season between a man of unimpaired semen and a woman whose generative organ, (menstrual) blood and womb are unvitiated—when, in fact, in the event of intercourse thus described, the individual soul (*jīva*) descends into the union of semen and (menstrual) blood in the womb in keeping with the (*karmically* produced) psychic disposition (of the embryonic matter)."[56] This seems to mean that conception coincides with the "descent" or presence of the spirit in the womb—that from the beginning the embryo is the spirit-matter composite that constitutes the human person. There seems to be no scope according to this seminal authority for drawing the distinction between human being and human person, with the implication that abortion at some early stage of pregnancy may be permissible.

In the minor tradition, however, the soul unites with the embryo some time AFTER conception. Here, it seems that grounds do exist for drawing a distinction between human being (the embryo before the union with the soul) and human person (the embryo after the union). The minor tradition is (perhaps uniquely) expressed in the *Garbha Upaniṣad* (circa 2d–3d century C.E.?), a minor Upaniṣad and hardly a recognised authority in such matters. The *Garbha Upaniṣad* has it that soul and embryo unite in the seventh month after conception:

> As a result of intercourse in due season, the embryo forms in the space of a night; within seven nights a bubble forms; in the period of a fortnight, there is a lump and by a month this becomes hard. In two months the head develops, in three months the region of the feet, and in the fourth month the ankles, stomach, and loins form. In the fifth month, the back and spine form; in the sixth month, nose, eyes, and ears develop. In the seventh month, (the foetus) is joined to the soul, and in the eighth month it is complete in every (part).[57]

It is important to point out that neither the *Garbha Upaniṣad*, in particular, nor the minor tradition, in general, ever explicitly draws a distinction analogous to that between human being and human person described earlier, either with or without reference to abortion. We cannot derive any conclusions about the permissiblity of abortion, therefore, from any argument which refers specifically to a time lapse between conception and ensoulment, based on the minor tradition.

But, it may be objected, one does not need to appeal to this kind of argument in the attempt to make a case for the permissibility of (early) abortion in our context. For if it can be shown that even according to the major tradition it is only relatively late in pregnancy—if at all—that the mark of ensoulment, viz., conscious experience, occurs, then it can be argued that BEFORE the appearance of this sign only the NECESSARY (not the sufficient) condition obtains for personhood in the embryo. In this instance, abortion may be permissible for reasons and in situations acknowledgedly not valid if and when the SUFFICIENT condition (viz., consciousness) does apply.

This is our cue for examining the evidence, in the classical tradition, as to whether the embryo/foetus has conscious experience or not. In fact, it was commonly believed that, at least in a relatively advanced stage of pregnancy, there is conscious experience in the womb. This awareness is invariably connected with the so-called *garbha-duḥkha* or sufferings of residence in the womb. The *Viṣṇu Purāṇa* says:

> An individual soul (*jantu*), possessing a subtle body (*sukumāratanu*), resides in his mother's womb (*garbha*), which is imbued with various sorts of impurity (*mala*). He stays there being folded in the membrane surrounding the foetus (*ulba*). . . . He experiences severe pains . . . tormented immensely by the foods his mother takes. . . . Incapable of extending (*prasāraṇa*) or contracting (*ākuñcana*) his own limbs and reposing amidst a mud of faeces and urine, he is in every way incommoded. He is unable to breathe. Yet, being endowed with consciousness (*sacaitanya*) and thus calling to memory many hundreds (of previous) births, he resides in his mother's womb with great pains, being bound by his previous deeds.[58]

The *Garbha Upaniṣad* elaborates on one aspect of this painful experience:

> Now (when the foetus) is complete in every aspect, it remembers its past births. Action pertains to what is done and not done, and (the foetus) thinks upon its good and bad deeds. Having surveyed (previous births from) thousands of different wombs, (it thinks): "Thus have I enjoyed various foods and suckled various teats. Again and again both the living and the dead are reborn. Alas! I am sunk in this ocean of sorrow and see no remedy. Whatever I've done, good or bad, for those about me—I alone must suffer the consequences, for they've gone on their way, suffering the fruits (of their own deeds). If ever I escape the womb I'll study the *Sāṃkhya-Yoga* which destroys evil and confers the reward of liberation. If ever I escape the womb I'll abandon myself to Śiva who destroys evil and confers the reward of liberation."[59]

But the trauma of birth—the squeezing in the vaginal passage and the impact of the air outside the mother's body (the so-called Vaiṣṇava Wind)—erases all memories and stupefies (*bālakaraṇa:* makes a child of!) the newborn.[60]

The *Suśruta Saṃhitā* is more specific as to when consciousness develops in the womb:

> In the first month (after conception) the embryo is formed, in the second . . . there results a compact mass. If this is globular (*piṇḍa*), it's a male,

> if longish (*peśī*) it's a female. . . . In the third month, five protuberances appear for the hands, legs and head, while the division of the other bodily limbs and sections is hardly visible (*sūkṣma*). In the fourth month, the division of these other limbs and sections appears clearly, while awareness as a distinct category (*cetanādhātu*) manifests itself in relation to the appearance of the foetus' heart. . . . Also in the fourth month, the foetus expresses desires in respect of sense-objects. . . . In the fifth month the coordinating sense (*manas*) becomes more aware, and in the sixth the intellect (*buddhi*) is manifest. In the seventh month, the division of the bodily limbs and sections is more defined; in the eighth month the life-force (*ojas*) concentrates. . . . In one or other of the ninth, tenth, eleventh, or twelfth months, birth takes place, or else (the pregnancy) is void.[61]

Note that nothing is said here to indicate that in its development the embryo undergoes a quantum leap, passing from one kind of human moral status (human being) to another (human person). On the contrary, in characteristic Hindu fashion, the language here is in terms of progressive MANIFESTATION, of a personhood previously only latent rather than origination of personhood *ab initio*.[62] The *Suśruta Saṃhitā* confirms this conclusion when, after describing the development of the foetus, it observes in the face of opposing views that the foetus undergoes an all-round (rather than sporadic) development from the very beginning.[63] For its part, the *Caraka Saṃhitā* implies that the conscious principle is active in the fertilised egg, directing its growth, right from conception.[64] Thus, in respect of the development of the unborn, the language of the manifestation of consciousness in traditional Hinduism cannot be and never has been taken to refer to qualitatively different moral statuses of the embryo/foetus. There is no scope here then for arguing for abortion in a traditional context.

The same stricture applies to the minor tradition, notwithstanding the time lapse it introduces between conception and ensoulment.[65] This hiatus, too, has never been used to distinguish qualitatively, in a moral sense, between one stage of the embryo and another, with or without abortion in mind. So, as noted before, we can deduce nothing positively concerning the permissibility of abortion on the basis of this hiatus. In point of fact, the overriding evidence of the classical texts as a whole speaks in favour of according the status of human personhood to the unborn throughout pregnancy, with consequent implications for (the impermissibility of) abortion, except in extreme circumstances (see earlier).

Other reasons, embracing both traditions, can be adduced for the standard view on abortion.

Linguistic Evidence

There is the argument from the negative evidence of the linguistic terms used to describe different stages in the development of the embryo.[66]

At no stage in pregnancy is the embryo/foetus designated by a particular term so as to indicate in any way that it is susceptible of abortion for reasons not obtaining when the embryo/foetus is differently designated. Further, while it is invariably some compound containing *bhrūṇa* (embryo/foetus) which is used to express the reprehensible act of abortion in the literature, *bhrūṇa* is never used, to the best of my knowledge, as a recognised term for designating a particular stage in the development of the embryo. Thus, there is no linguistic evidence to enforce a distinction positing different moral statuses in the unborn, or by implication, favouring abortion.

Karma and Rebirth

Another reason which made abortion unacceptable in traditional Hinduism was the belief in *karma* and rebirth, outlined earlier. This belief, in one or other of its variants, was firmly implanted in the Hindu psyche from very early times and had far-reaching consequences for Hindu practice. It militated against abortion, in that abortion could be regarded as thwarting the unfolding of the *karma* of both the unborn and the perpetrator(s) of the act. The unborn's *karma* matures through its prenatal and postnatal experiences, and abortion unnaturally terminates the possibility of this maturation. Abortion thus gravely affected the outworking of a person's destiny, the more so since it is generally believed that it was as a human being that one could act most effectively to achieve liberation from rebirth.[67]

An objection may be raised here. Why could not abortion be permissible as itself (unwittingly) predetermined by *karma*? The Hindus countered this objection by maintaining that the experience of free choice was not an illusion, that the law of *karma* did not abrogate the laws of *dharma*, of right living in accordance with freedom and responsibility. In other words, deliberate abortion as a free act violates *dharma* and, as such, is reprehensible. In Hindu tradition, the real distinction between "timely" and "untimely" death was recognised. If this distinction did not apply, if everything that happened (abortion included) could indiscriminately be put down to the predetermined unfolding of the *karmic* law, there would be no place for free, responsible action, and the law of *karma*, which is based on such action, would itself be subverted.

Caraka considers the issue raised by the objection and answers:

> If all life-spans were fixed (willy-nilly by the power of *karma*, abortion notwithstanding), then in search of good health none would employ efficacious remedies or verses, herbs . . . oblations . . . fastings . . . There would be no disturbed, ferocious, or ill-mannered cattle, elephants . . . and the like . . . no anxiety about falling from mountains or (into) rough, impassable waters; and none whose minds were negligent. . . . NO VIOLENT ACTS, NO ACTIONS OUT OF PLACE OR UNTIMELY (SUCH AS ABORTION). . . .

> For the occurrence of these and the like would not (freely) cause death if the term of all life were fixed and predetermined. Also, the fear of untimely death would not beset those creatures who did not practise the means for fending off fear of untimely death. Undertaking to employ the stories and thoughts of the great seers regarding the prolongation of life would be senseless. Even Indra could not (choose to) slay with his thunderbolt an enemy whose life span was fixed.[68]

Though a number of philosophical questions are begged in this passage, the point is that the decrees of *karma* and the freedoms of *dharma* were not regarded as incompatible in Hindu thought. Thus one could not justify abortion as the instrument of *karma* in the face of the clear condemnations of *dharma*.

The Embryo: A Symbol of Life

Again, the embryo in the womb was sacrosanct because it was a potent symbol of a dominant motif regulating the traditional Hindu view of life—that of birth, regeneration, new life, immortality. The theme of the primeval egg of creation from which the world of plurality emerges is a popular one in Hindu folklore. For example, we read in the *Mbh.*: "When all this (universe) was (originally) darkness, unillumined, covered on all sides by obscurity, the Great Egg arose, the sole imperishable seed of creatures. They say that at the beginning of an age this is the great, divine cause, and that on which (it rests) is revealed as the true Light, the eternal Brahman."[69] There are a number of variants of this image of the egg of creation in the scriptural texts.[70] The *Śatapatha Brāhmaṇa* informs us that in certain rituals the initiate was compared or associated with an embryo, no doubt because the latter was suggestive of new birth or life.[71] In the light of this symbolism, we can see why abortion was generally condemned in traditional Hinduism.

Social and Religious Reasons

A more practical reason for safeguarding the life of the embryo stemmed from the social and religious need to produce, especially male, offspring. Since Hindu society was, in the main, patriarchal, male progeny, in particular, were necessary not only to maintain social and economic stability (by a proper functioning of the caste system) but also for religious purposes (the performance of the priestly and domestic ritual, especially the *śrāddha* rite to ensure that deceased parents entered a satisfactory post-mortem existence). Great store was laid by the birth of a son (or sons—there was security in numbers) for this latter purpose.

In fact, the need to produce offspring for these reasons determined to a large extent the attitude of traditional (male-dominated) Hindu society to women. Women fulfilled their role by being wives and mothers, i.e., childbearers and child-rearers. The following quotations from the *MnS*, a seminal law text of our period, show the interplay of some of the ideas noted above: 1. "The husband, having entered his wife, is born here as an embryo, for that is the wifehood of the wife that he is born again of her"; 2. "As is he to whom a wife cleaves, so is the offspring. Therefore one should protect one's wife with care for the purity of one's progeny"; 3. "Women were made for child-bearing, men for continuing the line, hence public rites are enjoined in the Veda are to include the wife."[72]

A special point to note here is that the production of children was a public duty, rather than a purely individual expression of parental rights and choices. Indeed, one of the traditional debts the householder owed society was maintaining society's numbers by continuing the line in accordance with *dharma*. It would be unHindu, therefore, to regard procreation and concomitant issues (such as abortion) as a private concern of mother (or family) alone. One can understand how in this whole context then—that of the social, economic and religious issues—abortion, in general, was condemned.

Ahiṃsā

Finally, we may mention the influence of the principle of *ahiṃsā* or non-injury in Hindu tradition as a factor militating against the performance of abortion. While it is true that in Hinduism, in general, this principle never enjoyed the unambivalent status it had in the Jaina and Buddhist traditions (the *Bhagavad-Gītā,* for instance, may be regarded as a defence of just war undertaken out of selfless duty), it still exerted a powerful influence on the Hindu mind with reference to particularly vulnerable forms of life, such as the embryo. Revitalised in contemporary times by the example of M. K. Gandhi, this principle traditionally applied to all living (especially breathing) beings. It had a twofold aspect: negative, that is, avoiding violence in thought and deed; and positive, being well-disposed towards, in thought and deed.

Since abortion entailed the inflicting of (mental and) physical violence to the point of death on the unborn person, it flew in the face of the ingrained Hindu reverence for (the seed of) life. It ran counter to the Hindu genius to empathise and harmonise with natural forces and processes rather than to exploit and dominate them. This is a main feature of the rationale underlying *ahiṃsā*.

VI. Conclusion

Let us now conclude this chapter by summing up the main points of our study and by a brief comment on the contemporary scene in Hindu India. We begin by noting that this study has proceeded by way of a return to the sources. We have analysed our topic on the basis of orthodox Hindu Sanskrit texts falling within what has been described as the classical period, from an historical and philosophical point of view. What has been considered is the official teaching of the code-makers. No claim is being made that this study is significant sociologically for conclusions to be drawn, one way or another, as to what was really believed/practised concerning abortion by other nonregulative sections of the Hindu society of the times. Further, while it is true that this essay has not made use of modern relevant data, a textual treatment such as this is necessary, I submit, for the modern debate that is already emerging.[73] For it is typically Hindu to debate an important issue for life with reference to its traditional religious and moral roots. I venture to say that the topic of this essay has rarely, if ever, had the benefit of the study brought to bear here.

We may conclude from our study then, that from earliest times, especially in the formative classical period described, both in canonical and collaborative orthodox Hindu literature, abortion (viz., deliberately caused miscarriage as opposed to involuntary miscarriage) at any stage of pregnancy, has been morally condemned as violating the personal integrity of the unborn, save when it was a question of preserving the mother's life. No other consideration, social or otherwise, seems to have been allowed to override this viewpoint.

After outlining the traditional Hindu model of human personhood, we analysed the reasons for this stance on abortion and the moral status of the unborn. Irrespective of the moment of ensoulment in the womb, no distinction seems to have been made or enforced in the literature analogous to the human being/human person distinction in some western discussions with its bearing on the permissibility of (at least early) abortion. In other words, *de facto*, Hindu tradition has always accorded personal moral status to the embryo/foetus throughout pregnancy. Other reasons converge in shaping the accredited view: advanced conscious experience in the developed foetus; the absence of linguistic evidence endorsing the abortability of the embryo at one point in pregnancy rather than at another; the implications of the law of *karma* and rebirth; the dominant influence of the egg/seed motif as suggestive of new life; the need to preserve caste, line, and race, not to mention family; the importance of ensuring a good post-mortem existence for deceased parents by the performance of the *śrāddha* rite; and the reverence for the principle of *ahiṃsā*.

Note that these are not only rational reasons—social, religious, and cultural factors, in general, have played a large part in shaping the traditional Hindu attitude to the unborn. And so it must be in the formation of a genuinely human response. The point is that the classical attitude has grown in a distinctive cultural context and that the modern response to the issue under consideration will also grow out of that context, as well as be determined by the contemporary Indian context. One cannot argue simplistically, as some moralists would have it, that only timeless rational (as opposed to more widely cultural) factors should be brought to bear in this matter. In any case, what counts for the cogency of purely rational reasons/arguments for any people/group is often itself culturally determined. The Hindu attitude to abortion and the unborn is the result of a rich cultural matrix. It will continue to be so determined in the present and the future and only as such can contribute distinctively to the discussion on the topic in the world at large. In this respect, the traditional Hindu stress on the wider social and moral obligations attaching to pregnancy (not excluding those to the child-to-be and the father), rather than the making of pregnancy a matter exclusively of individual rights (especially of the mother), must be noted.[74]

Modern India, a secular democracy, permits abortion by law, under certain circumstances. No doubt this is a law availed of by some. Yet it is true to say that the issues relating to the moral status of the unborn and abortion have neither been aired nor even properly identified, in general, in Indian minds and literature. In public, the topic is by and large taboo. Illegal abortionists in the back street or the bush continue to ply their trade, often with dire consequences for their customers. To check exploitation of one kind or another in this matter, the issue must be thrown open.

In this chapter I have not sought to evaluate or to argue for or against any side. Rather, I have provided but a preliminary (and incomplete) historical and analytical study. Others are invited to continue the task.

Notes

1. I can illustrate this from my own experience. In preparation for a visit to two well-known universities in India, shortly after completing this chapter, I offered the present topic (among others) to the relevant departments for possible seminars/public lectures. I was not too surprised to discover that, in both cases, this particular topic was politely singled out for exclusion on "cultural" grounds. It so happened that soon after my return from India I was to visit a university in Canada and one in the United States. I made the same proposal; in both instances, this topic was singled out for presentation.
2. Unless the context requires otherwise, in this chapter no significant distinction is intended between the terms "embryo" and "foetus". Further, except where it is made clear to the contrary, our discussion applies specifically to the living, human embryo.
3. In theory, though not always in practice, the former are more authoritative than the latter.
4. See P. V. Kane's *History of Dharmaśāstra*. Poona: Bhandarkar Oriental Research Institute, 1968, vol. 1, pt 1, 2d. ed., pp. 22f.

5. "In the event of the miscarriage (*sraṃsana*) of the embryo (due observance of the purification ritual should be made for) as many a night as equals the months of pregnancy," *garbhamāsasamā rātrīḥ sraṃsane garbhasya.* For the Sanskrit text, see *The Gautama-Dharma-Sūtra* (WITH THE MITĀKṢARA, SANSKRIT COMMENTARY OF HARADATTA), ed. U. Chandra Pandey, Varanasi: Kashi Sanskrit Series, 172, 1966; p. 147. For an English translation, see THE SACRED BOOKS OF THE EAST, vol. 2, trans. G. Bühler, Oxford, 1879, p. xiv. 17. Unless stated otherwise, all translations from the Sanskrit in this chapter are my own.

6. See Kane, *Dharmaśāstra,* vol. 1, pt 1, 2d. ed., pp. 306f.

7. "In the event of miscarriage of the embryo (*garbhasrāva*) (the woman) is purified by (due observance of the ritual for) as many nights as correspond to the months (of pregnancy)," :*rātribhir māsatulyābhir garbhasrāve viśuddhyati.* Sanskrit text from *The Manusmṛti (with the Manvartha Muktāvali Commentary by Kullūka Bhaṭṭa),* ed. Pandit Gopala Sastri Nene, Benares: Kashi Sanskrit Series, 114, 1935, v. 66, p. 162.

8. See Kane, *Dharmaśāstra,* pp. 421f, esp. p. 443.

9. *garbhasrāve māsatulyā niśāḥ śuddhes tu kāraṇam.* Sanskrit text from *Yājñavalkyasmṛti of Yogīshwara Yājñavalkya with the Mitākṣarā Commentary of Vijñāneshwar,* ed. U. Chandra Pandey, Varanasi: Kashi Sanskrit Series, 178, 1967, p. 410.

10. *ā caturthād bhavet srāvaḥ pātaḥ pañcamaṣaṣṭayoḥ. ata ūrdhvaṃ prasūtiḥ syād daśāhaṃ sūtakaṃ bhavet.* Pandey, *Yājñavalkyasmṛti* p. 411. The *Suśruta Saṃhitā,* a seminal medical authority of our period, and about which more presently, appears to recall an earlier version of this tradition when it says of miscarriage: "Up until the fourth month there would emerge a 'discharge from the womb'; then, from the fifth and the sixth (month, we can speak of) the 'fall' of the (now) solidified body": *ā caturthāt tato māsāt prasraved garbhavicyutiḥ. tataḥ sthitaśarīrasya pātaḥ pañcamaṣaṣṭayoḥ.* See *Suśrutasaṃhitā,* trans. by Atrideva, Benares: Motilal Banarsidass, 2d. ed., 1957; *Nidānasthāna* VIII.10. p. 254. The rationale is given here, in the context of the traditional Hindu view on the development of the embryo, for describing miscarriage in early pregnancy by "flow" terms and in later pregnancy by "falling/dropping" terms, viz., the more or less liquified state of the embryonic matter.

11. A good example of the conflation of this important distinction, in translation at least, occurs in Kane when he writes, referring to different sources: "Abortion in the first four months of pregnancy . . . is called srāva" and so on. Not "abortion", in fact, but "miscarriage". See Kane, *Dharmaśāstra,* vol. 4, p. 275.

12. *viṣṇuṃ niṣiktapām* (*Ṛg Saṃhitā* VII.36.9) on which Sāyana comments: (this means) "the preserver of the infant-to-be": *niṣiktasya garbhasya rakṣitāram.* See also e.g., X.184.1, under which Sāyana glosses: "May Viṣṇu, the (all-) pervading deity, make the womb a place for the repose of the embryo": *viṣṇur vyāpako devo yoniṃ garbhādhānasthānaṃ kalpayatu karotu.*

13. Thus in the *Caraka Saṃhitā,* a classical medical text to which we shall return, we are informed that *Ṛg Saṃhitā* X.184.1 was used to invoke Viṣṇu in the ceremonies prior to conception (See the *jātisūtrīya śārīrasthāna* in *The Caraka Saṃhitā of Agniveśa (revised by Caraka and Dṛḍhabala),* ed. G. Pandeya,

Varanasi: Kashi Sanskrit Series, 194, pt. 1, 1969, 11. p. 818). In this respect Viṣṇu is to be contrasted with Nirṛti, the destroyer of order and life, including the embryo.

14. *marīcīr dhūmān praviśānu pāpmann udārān gaccota vā nīhārān nadīnāṃ phenān anu tān vinaśya bhrūṇaghni pūṣan duritāni mṛkṣva.* See *Atharvaveda (Śaunaka) with Pada-pāṭha and Sāyaṇācārya's Commentary,* ed. Vishva Bandhu, Vishveshvaranand Indological Series 14, pt. 2, Hoshiarpur: Vishveshvaranand Vedic Research Institute, 1961, p. 818.

15. For this, see Bloomfield's contribution to the *Journal of the American Oriental Society,* vol. 14 (under "Proceedings" for March 1894, pp. cxxii-cxxiii).

16. *hādbhutam abhijanitor jāyāyai garbhaṃ niravadhīd iti pāpmakad iti pāpī kīrttis tasmād dhenvanaḍuhayor nāśnīyāt* . . . III.1.2, vr. 21, from *The Śatapatha Brāhmaṇa (of the White Yajurveda in the Mādhyandina Recension),* ed. Pandit A. Chinnaswami Sastri and Pandit Pattabhirama Sastry, Benares: Kashi Sanskrit Series, 127, 1937, p. 200. It is interesting to note that, even though under IV.4.3.1f (ibid., p. 380) the text calls for atonement if it transpires that a pregnant cow has been killed instead of the requisite barren animal in the course of a particular ritual, there are (rare) instances in the *Śatapatha Brāhmaṇa* when the sacrificial slaughter of a pregnant cow is required (see V.4.4.8–10, ibid., p. 479, which pertains to the Rājasūya sacrifice or inauguration of the king. Here, perhaps the exceptional nature of the sacrifice requires an exceptionally symbolic victim. The king, symbolically identified through the sacrifice with the cow embryo, is seen to be the offspring of the land and of his people and thus the rightful inheritor of both).

17. Two of the most despised groups of outcastes.

18. *atra pitāpitā bhavati, mātāmātā, lokā alokāḥ, devā adevāḥ, vedā avedāḥ; atra steno' steno bhavati, bhrūṇahābhrūṇahā, cāṇḍālo' cāṇḍālaḥ, paulkaso 'paulkasaḥ, śramaṇo' śramaṇaḥ, tāpaso 'tāpasaḥ, ananvāgataṃ puṇyena, ananvāgataṃ pāpena, tīrṇo hi tadā sarvān śokān hṛdayasya bhavati,* IV.3.22. From *The Principal Upaniṣads* by S. Radhakrishnan, London: Allen & Unwin, 1953. Here we must note that from very early on in the literature the expressions *bhrūṇahatyā* /*bhrūṇahan* came to have two senses: killing an embryo, and killing a Brahmin (also, killer of the embryo/Brahmin). W. Gampert notes in his *Die Sühnezeremonien in der altindischen Rechtsliteratur,* Prag: Orientalisches Institut, 1939, pp. 62–3: "*Diese Sünde* (i.e., *Embryotötung*) *wurde ursprünglich nur mit* bhrūṇahatyā *bezeichnet; im Laufe der Zeit erfuhr dieser Ausdruck jedoch eine Erweiterung seiner Bedeutung, indem er auch die Tötung eines Brahmanen, insbesondere eines gelehrten, umfasste. Die Folge davon war, dass eine vollständige Vermischung der beiden Sünden Embryotötung und Brahmanentötung eintrat und es von da an oft ganz unklar ist, ob* bhrūṇahatyā (*bzw.* bhrūṇahan *zur Bezeichnung des Täters*) *nur die Embryotötung oder auch die Brahmanentötung bezeichnet*" (See also ensuing discussion). To go into reasons for this fusion of meanings would take us too far afield. Gampert himself does not discuss the matter. Sufficient for us to point out that in our own discussion (1) where both senses of the Sanskrit could apply, there are no grounds for saying that the sense which concerns us, viz. "killing/killer of the embryo," is not one of the main senses intended (indeed, the ambiguity may well be deliberate), and (2) instances often occur when there is no ambiguity in meaning, as the context makes clear.

19. *sa yo māṃ veda na ha vai tasya kena cana karmaṇā loko mīyate, na steyena na bhrūṇa-hatyayā, na mātṛ-vadhena, na pitṛ-vadhena.* See Radhakrishnan, *The Principal Upaniṣads,* p. 774.

20. See *La Mahā Nārāyaṇa Upaniṣad,* ed. and trans. J. Varenne, Paris: Publications de l'institut de Civilisation Indienne, 1960, vol. 1: *akāryakāry avakīrṇī steno bhrūṇahā gurutalpagaḥ* (159), *varuṇo apām aghamarṣaṇas tasmāt pāpāt pramucyate* (160); ibid., IV.p.44. See also, *corasya annaṃ navaśrāddhaṃ brahmahā gurutalpagaḥ* (436), *gosteyaṃ surāpānaṃ bhrūṇahatyāṃ tilāḥ śāntiṃ śamayantu svāhā* (437); ibid., X.p.104. Note that in the second reference the text distinguishes between killing the embryo (*bhrūṇahatyām*) and killer of a Brahmin (*brahmahā*), so that Varenne may be presuming too much in translating the *bhrūṇahā* of the FIRST reference by "celui qui tue un brahmane" (ibid., p. 45).

21. Ibid., vol. 1, pt. 1, pp. 112f.

22. *yāgasthasya kṣatriyasya vaiśyasya ca rajasvalāyāś cāntarvatnyāś cātrigotrāyāś cāvijñātasya garbhasya śaraṇāgatasya ca ghātanaṃ brahmahatyāsamānīti.* See the *Viṣṇusmṛti with the Commentary Keśavavaijayantī of Nandapaṇḍita,* ed. Pandit V. Krishnamacharya, Madras: Adyar Library Series, vol. 93, 1964, pt. 2, p. 478.

23. *ViDS* V.132: *brahmacārivānaprasthabhikṣugurviṇītīrthānusāriṇāṃ nāvikaḥ śaulkikaḥ śulkam ādadānaś ca; ViDS* pt. I, p. 120. The *MnS* exempts the pregnant woman from the fine for dropping litter. She is let off with a reprimand and is made to clean up the mess! viz., *āpadgato'thavā vṛddhā garbhiṇī bāla eva vā, paribhāṣaṇam arhanti tac ca śodhyam iti sthitiḥ; MnS* IX.283.p.325.

24. *panthā deyo brāhmaṇāya gobhyo rājabhya eve ca, vṛddhāya bhārataptāya garbhiṇyai durbalāya ca.* XIII.107.50; Poona edition.

25. *ayaṃ ca sakala eva sarvāsāṃ strīṇām agarbhiṇīnām abālāpatyānām ā caṇḍālaṃ sādhāraṇo dharmaḥ, Mit,* p. 37. Note that the text places even the worst untouchable (*ā caṇḍālam*) under the general recommendation of con-cremation. Untouchables were not necessarily beyond the pale of *dharma.*

26. *pūrṇam iva tailapātram asamkṣobhayatā'ntarvatnī bhavaty upacaryā,* Pandeya: *Caraka Saṃhitā* p. 825, vr. 22; See also the *jātisūtrīya* section of the *Śārīrasthāna.*

27. *bhrūṇahani hīnavarṇasevāyāṃ ca strī patati, GauDS* p. 214.

28. Kane: *Dharmaśāstra* vol. 1, pt. 1, pp. 53f.

29. *atha patanīyāni: steyam ābhiśastyaṃ puruṣavadho brahmojjhaṃ garbhaśātanaṃ mātuḥ pitur iti yonisambandhe sahāpatye strīgamanaṃ surāpānam asaṃyogasaṃyogaḥ.* See the *Āpastamba Dharmasūtra (with the Commentary Ujjwala by Śrī Haradatta Miśra),* ed. Pandit A. Chinnaswami Sastri and Pandit A. Ramanatha Sastri, Benares: Kashi Sanskrit Series, 93, 1932, I.7.21.7–8, p. 117. Haradatta comments: " 'abortion' here means killing the embryo by the use of herbs etc.": *auṣadhādiprayogena garbhasya vadho garbhaśātanam.*

30. *pāṣaṇḍam āśritānāṃ ca carantīnāṃ ca kāmataḥ, garbhabhartṛdruhāṃ caiva surāpīnāṃ yoṣitām, MnS* V.90.p.168. The commentator says of these, *udakakriyaurdhvadaihikaṃ nivarteta . . .*

31. Under *YjS* II.236; the *Mit.* makes this 100 *paṇas,* glossing the *YjS's śatadaṇḍabhāk* by *paṇaśataṃ daṇḍārhā;* see *Mit.*, p. 254.

32. *śastrāvapāte garbhasya pātane cottamo damaḥ, uttamo vādhamo vāpi puruṣastrīpramāpaṇe:* "The highest punishment is due for unjury with a weapon and for abortion; the highest or the lowest (depending on circumstances) for the murder of a man or a woman." According to the *Mit.*, the latter half of this statement means that "the highest or lowest punishment due is fixed for the murder of a man or a woman depending upon the virtue, conduct, and so on of the individual concerned:" *puruṣasya striyāś ca pramāpaṇe śīlavṛttādyapekṣyottamo vādhamo vā daṇḍo vyavasthita veditavyaḥ; Mit.* II.277. For further information about guilt and expiation relating to abortion, see Gampert: *Sühnezeremonien* Note that the kind of penalty incurred in the texts for abortion is different from the kind of penalty attaching to miscarriage. In the case of miscarriage, the woman only becomes ritually impure (see notes 5, 7, 9); the abortionist, however, is punished as a WRONGDOER (see *passim*) with one exception (to be noted in due course).

33. *Mit.* II.277, pp. 267–8.

34. See note 32.

35. *yathoktavādinaṃ dūtaṃ kṣetradharmarato nṛpah, yo hanyāt pitaras tasya bhrūṇahatyām avāpnuyuḥ.* See also, e.g., *Mbh.* XII.20.8.

36. *abhikāmāṃ striyaṃ yas tu gamyāṃ rahasi yācitaḥ, nopaiti sa ca dharmeṣu bhrūṇahety ucyate buddhaih. Mbh.* I.78.33. See also I.78.32.

37. *kārṣṇaṃ vedam imaṃ vidvāñ śrāvayitvārtham aśnute, bhrūṇahatyākṛtaṃ cāpi pāpaṃ jahyān na saṃśayaḥ. Mbh.* I.1.205. See also I.56.18.

38. *evaṃ caiva naraśreṣṭha rakṣyā eva dvijātayaḥ, svaparāddhān api hi tān viṣayān te samutsṛjet. abhiśastam api hy eṣāṃ kṛpāyīta viśāṃpate, brahmaghne gurutalpe ca bhrūṇahatye tathaiva ca. Mbh.* XII.56.31–2. Note, in reference to note 18, that here, too, a clear distinction is made between slaying the Brahmin and slaying the embryo.

39. *ajñātaṃ dhṛtarāṣṭrasya yatnena mahatā tataḥ, sodaraṃ pātayāmāsa gāndhārī duḥkhamurcchitā. tato jajñe māṃsapeśī lohāṣṭhīleva saṃhatā Mbh.* I.107.11–12a. Note the use of the causative *pātayāmāsa* (caused [the foetus] to fall). Gāndhārī's is a deliberate act, but in view of the mitigating circumstance of her desperation, this less harsh expression is used for abortion in contrast to the unvarnished *bhrūṇahatyā.*

40. *sā sicyamānā aṣṭhīlā abhavac chatadhā tadā, aṅguṣṭhaparvamātrāṇāṃ garbhāṇāṃ pṛthag eva tu. Mbh.* I.107.19.

41. See notes 19, 20, 29.

42. See under *Abortion: Moral Evaluation in Smṛti (B).*

43. See note 25 which pertains to ALL wives, including the Cāṇḍāla, EXCEPT those who are pregnant or have young children to care for.

44. *nāto'nyat kaṣṭamam asti yayā mūḍhagarbhaśalyoddharaṇam, atra hi . . . karma kartavyaṃ sparśena . . . ekahastena garbhaṃ garbhiṇīṃ cāhiṃsatā;* Atrideva: *Suśrutasaṃhitā,* "Cikitsāsthāna" XV.3, p. 448.

45. *jivati tu garbhe sūtikāgarbhanirharaṇe prayateta;* ibid., *sū.* 5.

46. *dāryamāṇo hi (garbho) jananīm ātmānaṃ caiva ghātayet. aviṣahye vikāre tu śreyo garbhasya pātanaṃ, na garbhiṇyā viparyāsas tasmāt prāptaṃ na hāpayet;* ibid., *sū.* 10–11.

47. Note the term used, *pātanam* (causing the fall of the foetus), not *bhrūṇahatyā* (slaying the embryo) and the like, to indicate that this deed is had recourse to only in extreme circumstances. It is unjustified then to diminish the gravity of abortion for Suśruta by stating, as in the following extract, that he "recommends" abortion for a wider range of cases: ". . . Suśruta recommends abortion in certain cases. When the foetus is known to be defective, or damaged beyond repair, and there is no hope for a normal birth, surgical removal is prescribed. . . . Craniotomic operations, involving the destruction and subsequent removal of the foetus, are prescribed in certain cases of this nature"; *Suśruta Saṃhitā (A Scientific Synopsis)* by P. Ray, H. Gupta and M. Roy, New Delhi: Indian National Science Academy, 1980, p. 22. Such laisser-aller cannot be justified textually.

48. In this light, it is interesting to consider reference 17 in the text.

49. *kulakṣaye praṇaśyanti kuladharmāḥ sanātanāḥ, dharme naṣṭe kulaṃ kṛtsnam adharmo'bhibhavaty uta. adharmābhibhavāt kṛṣṇa praduṣyanti kulastriyaḥ, strīṣu duṣṭāsu vārṣṇeya jāyate varṇasaṃkaraḥ. saṃkaro narakāyaiva kulaghnānāṃ kulasya ca, patanti pitaro hy eṣāṃ luptapiṇḍodakakriyāḥ. dosair etaiḥ kulaghnānāṃ varnasaṃkarakārakaiḥ, utsādyante jātidharmāḥ kuladharmāś ca śāśvatāḥ. utsannakuladharmāṇāṃ manuṣyāṇāṃ janārdana, narake niyataṃ vāso bhavatīty anuśuśruma. Mbh.* (Poona edition) VI.23.40–44. Elsewhere in the *Mbh.*, Bhīṣma says to (king) Yudhiṣṭhira: "He who would seek the death of the king should die an exemplary death—so too the Ājīvaka, the thief and the miscegener": *rājño vadhaṃ cikīrṣed yas tasya citro vadho bhavet, ājīvakasya stenasya varṇasaṃkarakasya ca.* XII.86.21.

50. See, e.g., *MnS* X.1f. For a fuller discussion see Kane, *Dharmaśāstra* vol. 2, pt. 2, 2d. ed., ch. 2, pp. 50–104.

51. The same protection was extended to the embryo of an adulterous union, as we see from the following: "In the event of adultery, purity (of the woman occurs) in her season (viz., during the menses, if she has not conceived). If she is with child, she is to be abandoned; (similarly) when a woman slays the embryo or her husband or (commits some other) grave transgression": *vyabhicārād ṛtau śuddhir garbhe tyāgo vidhīyate; garbhabhartṛvadhādau ca tathā mahati pātake. YjS* I.72, p. 28. The juxtaposition of adultery and abortion above does not exclude condemnation of the latter when it was the consequence of the former.

52. The *Caraka Saṃhitā* is said to contain the substance of a comprehensive medical teaching given by the god Indra to a group of seers. One of these, Ātreya Punarvasu, committed the teaching to six disciples, of whom one again, Agniveśa, composed a treatise of the teaching. Caraka, finally, figures as the authoritative redactor of Agniveśa's text. His work, the *Caraka Saṃhitā,* which is said to have been unfinished, was apparently later revised and completed by another savant, Dṛḍhabala. The text itself proceeds, for the most part, by way of a discourse between Ātreya Punarvasu, Agniveśa, and others. Though the received Caraka-Dṛḍhabala version is usually dated between 200–500 C.E., there seems to be no doubt that it represents a medical tradition whose roots dig far deeper into

the past. There is much scholarly dispute concerning the roles Caraka, Dṛḍhabala, and perhaps others have played in constructing the received *Saṃhitā,* but for our purposes this debate is irrelevant. Suffice it to say that the *Caraka Saṃhitā* embodies the standard Hindu outlook of the classical period on the conception, nature, and development of the human foetus. For a resume and a bibliography of the origin and composition of the *Caraka Saṃhitā,* see M. G. Weiss's contribution, "Caraka Saṃhitā on the doctrine of Karma," in *Karma and Rebirth in Classical Indian Traditions,* ed. W. D. O'Flaherty, Berkeley: University of California Press, 1980, pp. 93–4.

53. *niṣkriyaṃ ca svatantraṃ ca vaśinaṃ sarvagaṃ vibhuṃ, vadanty ātmānam ātmajñāḥ kṣetrajñaṃ sākṣiṇaṃ tathā.* Pandeya, *Caraka Saṃhitā,* ch. 1, *sū.* 5, p. 690.

54. *garbhātmā hy antarātmā . . . tam . . . ācakṣate śāśvatam arujam ajaram amaram akṣayam abhedyam acchedyam aloḍyaṃ viśvarūpaṃ viśvakarmāṇam avyaktam anādim anidhanam akṣaram api.* Pandeya, *Caraka Saṃhitā,* ch. 3, sū. 8, p. 743.

55. *tatra śarīraṃ nāma cetanādhiṣṭhānabhūtaṃ pañcamahābhūtavikārasamudāyātmakaṃ samayogavāhi.* Pandeya, *Caraka Saṃhitā* ch. 6, *sū.* 4, p. 787. "The five elementals" are the fundamental forms of earth, water, fire, air, and ether constitutive of *prakṛti* or the material principle which unfolds from its subtle, unmanifest state into the material world as we experience it.

56. *puruṣasyānupahataretasaḥ striyāś cāpraduṣṭayoniśoṇitagarbhāśayāyā yadā bhavati saṃsargaḥ ṛtukāle, yadā cānayos tathāyukte saṃsarge śukraśoṇitasaṃsargam antargarbhāśayagataṃ jīvo'vakrāmati sattvasaṃprayogāt tadā garbho'bhinirvartate.* Pandeya, *Caraka Saṃhitā* ch. 3, *sū.* 3, p. 737. "in due season": in the law texts, intercourse was permitted from the third/fourth day after the appearance of the menses till the sixteenth day. "The union of semen and (menstrual) blood": it was believed that the procreative factor from the woman's side was the menstrual blood. For a discussion of the symbolism/interplay of procreative terms and elements in traditional Hinduism, see W. D. O'Flaherty, "Sexual Fluids," in *Women, Androgynes, and Other Mythical Beasts,* Chicago: Univ. of Chicago Press, 1980, ch. 2.

57. *ṛtukāle prayogād ekarātroṣitaṃ kalilaṃ (kalalaṃ?) bhavati, saptarātroṣitaṃ budbudaṃ bhavaty, ardhamāsābhyantareṇa piṇḍo bhavati, māsābhyantareṇa kaṭhino bhavati, māsadvayena śiraḥ kurute, māsatrayeṇa pādapradeśo bhavaty, atha caturthe māse'ṅgulyajaṭharakaṭipradeśo bhavati, pañcame māse pṛṣṭhavaṃśo bhavati, ṣaṣṭhe māse nāsākṣiṇīśrotrāṇi bhavanti, saptame māse jīvena saṃyukto bhavaty, aṣṭame māse sarvasaṃpūrṇo bhavati.* See, "The Garbha Upaniṣad" in the Ānandāśrama Sanskrit Series, vol. 29, 1895, p. 161. "(the foetus) is joined to the soul": thus, *jīvena saṃyukto bhavati.* But the commentator, Nārāyaṇa, glosses this as: *Jīvaliṅgena* (*saṃyukto* . . .), i.e., is joined TO THE MARK of the soul—which is consciousness. If this interpretation is correct, then the implication is that CONSCIOUSNESS, not ensoulment, occurs in the seventh month. Ensoulment may well have taken place at conception. In this event, the minor tradition collapses into the major.

58. Quoted from Minoru Hara, "A Note on the Buddha's Birth Story," in *Indianisme et Bouddhisme* (Mélanges offerts à Mgr. Étienne Lamotte), Louvain-la-Neuve: Publications de l'institut Orientaliste de Louvain, 23, 1980, pp. 148–9. Hara gives another quotation, to similar effect, from the *Garuḍa Purāṇa;* p. 151.

59. *atha . . . sarvalakṣaṇasaṃpūrṇo bhavati pūrvajātīḥ smarati. kṛtākṛtaṃ ca karma bhavati śubhāśubhaṃ ca karma vindati. nānāyonisahasrāṇi dṛṣṭvā caiva tato mayā, āhārā vividhā bhuktāḥ pītāś ca vividhāḥ stanāḥ. jātasyaiva mṛtasyaiva janma caiva punaḥ punaḥ, aho duḥkhodadhau magno na paśyāmi pratikriyām. yan mayā parijanasyārthe kṛtaṃ karma śubhāśubham ekākī tena dahyāmi gatās te phalabhoginaḥ. yadi yonyāṃ pramuñcāmi sāṃkhyaṃ yogaṃ samabhyaset, aśubhakṣayakartāraṃ phalamuktipradāyinam. yadi yonyāṃ pramuñcāmi taṃ prapadye maheśvaram, aśubhakṣayakartāraṃ phalamuktipradāyinam. Garbha Upaniṣad:* Ānandāśrama p. 162–3. The foetus' rueing of rebirth and of the deeds perpetuating it, as also the resolution to take steps to avoid the process, is a recurrent theme in popular Sanskrit literature. See Hara for more examples.

60. See Hara, "Buddha's Birth Story," esp. pp. 149f.

61. *tatra prathame māsi kalalaṃ jāyate; dvitīye . . . (abhiprapacyamānānāṃ mahābhūtānāṃ) saṃghāto ghanaḥ saṃjāyate. yadi piṇḍaḥ pumān, strī cet peśī . . . tṛtīye hastapādaśirasāṃ pañcapiṇḍakā nirvartante'ṅgapratyaṅgavibhāgaś ca sūkṣmo bhavati. caturthe sarvāṅgapratyaṅgavibhāgaḥ pravyakto bhavati, garbhahṛdayapravyaktibhāvāc cetanādhātur abhivyakto bhavati . . . garbhaś caturthe māsy abhiprāyam indriyārtheṣu karoti . . .* (*sū.* 18). *pañcame manaḥ pratibuddhataraṃ bhavati, ṣaṣṭhe buddhiḥ. saptame sarvāṅgapratyaṅgavibhāgaḥ pravyaktataraḥ, aṣṭame'sthirī bhavaty ojaḥ . . . navamadaśamaikādaśadvādaśānām anyatam asmin jāyate, ato'nyathā vikārībhavati. sū.* 30; Atrideva: *Suśrutasaṃhita, Sārīrasthāna,* ch. 3, pp. 299 & 301, "in relation to the appearance of the foetus' heart": it was believed that the heart was the bodily abode of consciousness. The *Caraka Saṃhitā* does not differ substantially in its description of embryonic development. Hara, "Buddha's Birth Story," p. 154, ft. nt. 49, points out that in the *Purāṇas* it was generally held that foetal consciousness appeared from the seventh to the ninth month and notes (p. 157, ft. nt. 71) that the first reference "in Sanskrit literature to prenatal experience and memory of previous births is found in Rig Veda 4.27.1 (Vāmadeva), and Aitareya Upaniṣad 4.6." There is some doubt concerning the interpretation of the *Ṛg Vedic* reference as bearing on the memory of previous births.

62. Note the frequency in the Sanskrit (see note 61) of terms intimating a transition from an unmanifest to a manifest state: *sūkṣma, pravyakta, abhivyakta.* Also, there is nothing in this extract of the so-called preformation theory—influential in the West in the 17th century—according to which the fertilised egg was an homunculus, or miniature human, complete with tiny arms, legs, head, and so on who simply grew in size as pregnancy progressed.

63. "'All the limbs and sections of the body grow simultaneously' says Dhanvantari (Suśruta's reputed teacher)": *sarvāṇy aṅgapratyaṅgāni yugapat saṃbhavantīty āha dhanvantariḥ.* Atrideva: *Suśruta Saṃhitā, sū.* 32, p. 302. The *Caraka Saṃhitā* has it that "the senses, limbs and members (of the embryo) develop simultaneously": *evam asyendriyāṇy aṅgāvayavāś ca yaugapadyenābhinirvartante. Śārīrasthāna,* ch. 4, *sū.* 14, p. 762.

64. "There (in the fertilised egg) the conscious principle with the coordinating sense as its instrument, is *already* working towards the realisation of the (various) qualities (of the individual)": *tatra* pūrvaṃ *cetanādhātuḥ sattvakaraṇo guṇagrahaṇāya pravartate . . . . Śārīrasthāna,* ch. 4, *sū.* 8, p. 759.

65. But note our comment on Nārāyaṇa's gloss in note 57.

66. Hara, "Buddha's Birth Story," p. 154, gives a standard list, apparently mainly of Buddhist origin.

67. In theory, the different versions of the rebirth belief allowed for a person's rebirth, on the one hand, in animal and plant form, on the other, as celestials or gods (*devas*). In practice, however, the various texts, including the theological treatises of thinkers like Śaṃkara, Rāmānuja, and Madhva, are preoccupied with the nature, ethics, and destiny of the human person and imply that a qualitative distinction exists between human and (at least) animal and vegetative life. A corollary of this implication, usually taken for granted and not given due philosophical analysis, is that it is in its human form that the soul can most effectively seek liberation.

68. Quotation taken from M. G. Weiss, "Caraka Saṃhitā on Karma," p. 95, (see note 52). Emphasis and words in brackets have been added.

69. *niṣprabhe'smin nirāloke sarvatas tamasāvṛte, bṛhad aṇḍam abhūd ekaṃ prajānāṃ bījam akṣayam. yugasyādau nimittaṃ tan mahad divyaṃ prackṣate, yasmiṃs tac chrūyate satyaṃ jyotir brahma sanātanạm. Mbh.* I.1.27–8.

70. See, e.g., *Śatapatha Brāhmaṇa* XI.1.6,1–2; VI.1.2.,1–2; *Maitrī* Up., vi. 8; *MnS* I.8f.

71. E.g., *Śatapatha Brāhmaṇa* III.1.3.28, where the sacrificial fire becomes the womb (*yoni*) of the sacrifice, and the initiate (*dikṣita*) the embryo (*garbha*); pp. 203–4, Pt. I.

72. 1. *patir bhāryāṃ saṃpraviśya garbho bhūtveha jāyate. jāyāyās tad dhi jāyātvaṃ yad asya jāyate punaḥ. MnS* IX.8, p. 287. Here reference is being made to the "rebirth" of the husband in his progeny. 2. *yādṛśaṃ bhajate hi strī sutaṃ sūte tathāvidham, tasmāt prajāviśuddhyarthaṃ striyaṃ rakṣet prayatnataḥ. MnS* IX.9, p. 287. 3. *prajanārthaṃ striyaḥ sṛṣṭāḥ santanārthaṃ ca mānavāḥ, tasmāt sādhārano dharmaḥ śrutau patnyā sahoditaḥ. MnS* IX.96, p. 298.

73. See, e.g., Veena Das' short but pregnant(!) article, "The Debate on Abortion," in SEMINAR, Nov. 1983, pp. 31–35.

74. In this context, Ms. Das writes: ". . . we have been tricked by modern philosophers into thinking that the morality of abortion involves strictly the relation of a WOMAN to the foetus. In fact this dyadic relationship is embedded into a number of relationships involving not only the responsibility of a genitor to the embryo/foetus, but also the relationship of adult men and women. Further, this arrangement of relationships involves the rest of society. Without a discussion of the responsibility of society (either through the State or other agencies) towards the embryo, the foetus, and the infant as also towards those who are charged with caring for them, a discussion on the morality of abortion is incomplete." "Debate on Abortion," p. 34.

3. Euthanasia: Traditional Hindu Views and the Contemporary Debate

KATHERINE K. YOUNG

I. Introduction

THE EXTREME debilitation of advanced old age and severe illness have plagued human beings whose awareness and self-definition encompass both the idea of death and the "marker events"[1] that signal the dying process. How human beings have dealt with such awareness and experience has varied from epoch to epoch, culture to culture, person to person. Heroically living out the natural life span despite suffering, suicide to eliminate the difficult dying process, and murder whether by compassionate or selfish motives have all been human responses to these phenomena.

The history of the concept of euthanasia is closely associated with human dilemmas involved in advanced old age and severe illness. In classical Greece, the term meant the good death (*eu-*, good and *thanatos*, death)[2] and referred primarily to the mode of dying,[3] an easy or painless death associated with drinking hemlock.[4] "In Graeco-Roman antiquity, there was a generally recognized 'freedom to leave' that permitted the sick and despondent to terminate their lives, sometimes with outside help" (Gruman 1978, 261). Thus, the ancient view of euthanasia in the West was close to suicide, in that it was voluntary and self-imposed, although it may have been abetted, especially through provision of poison. Trowell, for example, thinks that some physicians in the Roman empire "did assist suicide, and even murder, by the issue of lethal drugs" and that the "Hippocratic oath and the oath of Asaph arose as protests against this practise" (1973, 8).

After such Jewish and Christian thinkers as Josephus, Augustine, and Aquinas[5] discouraged the practise of "active" euthanasia with their insistence on the natural life span, the term came to mean an "easy death" by leading a temperate life or by cultivating an acceptance of mortality. In the seventeenth century, however, "with Francis Bacon's *Advancement of Learning* (1605), 'euthanasia' increasingly came to connote specifically measures taken by the physician, including the possibility of hastening death" (Gruman 1978, 261). It is with the latter definition that the modern debate has emerged. Based on the idea of active intervention, the primary meaning is now compassionate murder (Trowell 1973, 13–22).

There are Western ethicists today who think that compassionate murder may be a moral act. The arguments proceed in a number of ways. Some challenge the Christian idea of the sanctity of life as an absolute principle by arguing that it is a "principle . . . valid most of the time (*in pluribus*), but in a particular instance (*in aliquo particulari*) it may not be applicable" (Maquire 1973, 195). Some argue that, while human life is a fundamental value and is to be protected, considerations of the quality of life also are to be entertained. Others challenge the Christian acceptance of suffering for its redemptive value and argue that life must be lived with dignity and comfort, including an easy or painless death. Still others challenge the definition of murder as the "killing of the innocent" and argue that murder is unjust killing; in this way scope is created for euthanasia as just or mercy killing. Then, too, there are ethicists who challenge religious or legal authority to forbid euthanasia by arguing that each individual is the absolute master of decisions regarding his/her own destiny.

Ethicists have debated the merits of compassionate murder. The term euthanasia itself has been delimited in recent years to provide greater precision for the discussion at hand, as new medical circumstances emerge or reflection on various issues becomes refined. While the process of legal definition making is far from over, there is a growing consensus in the West that the term euthanasia is to be reserved for the concept of compassionate murder in medically defined cases of terminal illness, which involves the medical profession in the active killing of the patient given due process of decision making.[6] It has been argued that euthanasia is to be distinguished, on the one hand, from homicide (culpable or inculpable) and, on the other hand, from situations of withdrawal of treatment, pain relief that may result in death, abetting suicide, and suicide proper. Hence, greater specificity is being given to the term euthanasia at the present, though different points are still debated and different legal systems may yet handle the issue in different ways. While it is becoming increasingly common in Western hospitals to accept withdrawal of treatment as a way of hastening death in situations of terminal illness, it is rare to accept such active intervention as administering poison by a physician.[7] Thus, whereas a distinction used to be made between inactive and active euthanasia or between omission and commission, now the distinction is between withdrawal of treatment and euthanasia as compassionate murder. The former is usually permissible in certain circumstances; the latter, even with its new technical restriction, remains largely unacceptable in the West.

This brief overview of the history of the term euthansia suggests that while euthanasia was related to the phenomenon of suicide in the Graeco-Roman world, it is now viewed as closer to murder, which is not to say that the conceptual boundaries of euthanasia in both these periods were not distinguished from the two extremes and in varying degrees invested with legitimacy. The change in the meaning of euthanasia, however, presents certain difficulties when one takes up the task of historical and cross-cultural studies. If we were to take today's emergent definition of euthanasia, with its technical insistence on medically defined cases of terminal illness and its circumscribed meaning of a doctor actively killing a patient on compassionate grounds, given due process of decision making, then, by definition, we would be hard pressed to find equivalent situations in the past and in other premodern societies. The contemporary definition excludes a pre-technological approach to medicine, especially the process of dying, not to mention different value systems.

When we turn to reflection on euthanasia in classical India, our task is made possible if we use, for hermeneutical purposes, the archaic meaning of euthanasia as "freedom to leave," which permitted the sick and despondent to terminate their lives. An alternative working definition for this historical study is self-willed death with reference to the extreme debilitation of advanced old age and the seemingly terminal nature of disease. Utilizing these definitions, we have sufficient scope to discover what were analogies in classical India to euthanasia in the Graeco-Roman world. The classical Indian view remained operant for a number of centuries (unlike the discontinuity in the West regarding the practise and definition of euthanasia). Recovery of the classical Indian view will be a major step in understanding the history of this phenomenon in India, how it differs from the history of euthanasia in the West, and how it may inform the contemporary discussion of termination of treatment and euthanasia today.

Death has been described as a central concern not only of Indian philosophy and religion but also of Indian sociology:

> as a source of Indian religious thought, death is probably unsurpassed; no matter which historical period or cultural level one chooses to examine, concepts lead to or from the problems it presents. . . . In the social world, if purity and impurity have anything to do with the way Hindus perceive

> and organize it, death is all the more central because it is the single most polluting human experience. And even if the pure/impure dichotomy is not the organizing principle of Hindu life, an opposition between death and life may be.
>
> (Blackburn 1985, 255)

When one approaches the topic of death in the classical Indian context, one encounters three basic types of death: natural, unnatural (being killed), and self-willed (killing oneself).

With reference to natural death we find that there was a strong Brahmanical (Hindu) prescription to live a hundred years or at least to the end of the natural life span. The funeral or *śrāddha* rites were performed for those who died a natural death. Those men who died naturally became the ancestors who were sustained through the offerings, ostensibly until they were reborn (though the offerings also ensured that they became gods (*viśvadeva*) as part of the process, thereby creating a double buffer against the idea of death as annihilation).

Unnatural death by being killed in battle, by murder or by accident was viewed as violent and not to be marked by *śrāddha*. Such death, however, was not necessarily perceived negatively, for it will be argued below that violent death, especially that of a warrior killed in battle, was religiously powerful, for it led to heaven or deification. (This idea is echoed even today in contemporary folk cults, which deify victims of murder or accident.)

Besides natural death and unnatural violent death, there also developed an acceptance of some forms of self-willed death. This category of self-willed death included three different types: suicide; what we shall term heroic, voluntary death (*mors voluntaria heroica*); and religious, self-willed death (*mors voluntaria religiosa*). By way of introduction, these three types may be distinguished by the following features. Suicide, which was prohibited, was self-willed death prompted by passion, depression, or uncontrollable circumstance. *Mors voluntaria heroica,* found mainly in the milieu of the warriors in ancient times, was: (1) a way to avoid calamity, as when a warrior avoided capture and a woman avoided rape or slavery by a conquerer through self-willed death; (2) a substitute for heroic death in battle that resulted in heaven; and (3) a way to allow peaceful succession to the throne. Closely related both historically and conceptually to heroic, self-willed death was *mors voluntaria religiosa*. The latter emphasized the religious dimension (heaven, liberation, or *dharma:* duty and social order based on religious principles). Religious, self-willed death was found outside the warrior milieu, though it drew from this context. Moreover, it was carefully distinguished from suicide, that is, passionate, self-willed death for reasons neither heroic nor religious.

The *Amarakośa*, which is written in the early classical period, places the category of death in the semantic domain (*varga*) of the warriors (Ksatriyas); after citing thirty terms for killing (*vadha*), it gives ten terms for natural death (*maraṇa*) and seven terms for dead (*mṛta*). While there is no term for self-willed death in this text, we shall argue below that reference to suicide, literally one who kills the self (*ātmahan*), makes its textual appearance in the Upaniṣads and early Buddhism and may be related to a critique of heroic, self-willed death which was beginning to occur in Vedic society. *Ātmahatyā* and *ātmaghāta* become the technical terms for suicide by the late classical period. The technical terms for the category of heroic and religious self-willed death, however, do not emerge until the Indian vernacular languages with the compounds *icchāmaraṇa* and *iṣṭamṛtyu* (literally death that is willed or desired); nonetheless, the *concept,* if not the technical term, exists by the time of the *Mahābhārata: naiṣa mṛtyuraniṣṭo no niḥṣṛtānām gṛhātsvayam* (for us who have voluntarily renounced our home, this death [by refusing to escape the forest fire] is not "not willed" (*aniṣṭa*) (MBh. 15.49.26). The implication is that the death is *iṣṭamṛtyu* or [self-] willed death, that is, desired death which is not evil, for the passage goes on to praise dying through fire, water, or wind (i.e. by jumping through air) by a hermit. (See Note 15 below for full discussion of this passage.) The category of *iṣṭamṛtyu* is also foreshadowed in several more specific terms found in classical Sanskrit or early Prakrit, which literally refer to the mode of dying yet by context indicate self-willed death, which is legitimate unlike suicide which is illegitimate: thus, *mahāprasthāna* (setting out on the great journey, departing this life, dying), *samādhimaraṇa* (death while in meditation), *prāyopaveśana* (abstaining from food and awaiting in a seating posture the approach of death), and the Jaina equivalent of *prāyopavésana*, which is called *sallekhanā.* To these specific terms we may add a number of descriptions that point to the acceptance if not desirability of self-willed death by burning, drowning, or jumping. Given this evidence of the phenomenon of self-willed death, the heroic and religious dimensions of which will become apparent in this study, introduction of the categories of *mors voluntaria heroica* and *mors voluntaria religiosa* as distinguished from suicide are valuable to facilitate the discussion of euthanasia.

The present analysis necessitates an historical treatment to see how these categories developed and where the topic of euthanasia is to be situated in the more general discussion of self-willed death. Different historical periods had very different understandings of the importance of the natural life span and the acceptability of heroic, voluntary death and religious, self-willed death. To illumine these historical vicissitudes with specific reference to the topic of euthanasia, it is necessary to understand not only the major shifts of the Brahmanical/Hindu Weltanschauung through the main epochs, but also how they related to and are informed by the dynamic interaction with Jainism and Buddhism. To capture the salient features of the evolving view of euthanasia, we shall look primarily to relevant passages in Sanskrit *śruti* and *smṛti* texts, though on several occasions we shall make reference to Jaina and Buddhist works.

Before we begin the historical treatment of our topic, five general observations may be made:

1. Much sympathy was expressed in classical India for euthanasia in the sense of "freedom to leave" by one suffering from a seemingly incurable disease or by one facing very debilitating old age.
2. Accordingly, euthanasia, belonged to the category of self-willed death and was never formally viewed as mercy killing of another person. Once there was a formal public declaration of the intent to perform self-willed death, helping the person was allowed. The individual's choice and willpower to implement it was therefore mandatory when euthanasia was accepted in the premodern Indian context.
3. The phenomenon of euthanasia was intimately related to the larger categories of heroic and religious self-willed death, which, in turn, were related to the yet broader context of violence and nonviolence in Indian society and religion.
4. Although there was positive evaluation of euthanasia in classical Hinduism, strong criticism developed by the 10th century C.E., which suggests that abuse occurred either of euthanasia proper or of other forms of heroic and religious, self-willed death to which it was closely associated, despite the attempt to define parameters.
5. The Indian Penal Code, based on British law at the time of the Rāj, views suicide as a criminal act. Because suicide has been interpreted as inclusive of all forms of self-willed death, euthanasia became illegal with the advent of British law in India.

A challenge to the Indian Penal Code's ruling on suicide was made by Justice T. K. Tukol in a series of lectures, to the L. D. Institute of Indology, published under the title *Sallekhanā is Not Suicide* (1976). While commentators on the Indian Penal Code have included the case of religious fasting to death among the forms of suicide, Justice Tukol argued that such fasting to death (*sallekhanā; samādhimaraṇa*) is not suicide:

> *upasarge durbhikṣe jarasi rujāyāṁ ca niḥpratīkāre|*
> *dharmāya tanuvimocanamāhuḥ sallekhanāmāryāḥ||*

> The wise ones say that *sallekhanā* is giving up the body when there is calamity (*upasarga*), [suffering from] famine (*durbhikṣā*), old age and decay (*jaras*), painful disease (*ruja*), and incurable disease (*niḥpratīkāra*) for the sake of *dharma*.

antarkriyādhikaranaṁ tapaḥ phalaṁ sakaladarśinaḥ stuvate|
tasmādyāvadvibhavaṁ samādhimaraṇe prayatitavyam||

All systems of religion praise the result of austerities (*tapas*) which is control of mind and action; therefore, one should try to attain dignity/emancipation from existence (*vibhava*) in *samādhimaraṇa*.

These two verses (*Ratna-karaṇḍaka-śrāvakācara* 22–23; text quoted by Tukol 1976, 107; translation here by K. Young) describe the Jaina forms of voluntary death (*sallekhanā*) as legitimate responses to debilitating old age and incurable disease. It is noted that other Indian religious systems have a similar method of death by austerities and meditation, presumably in the same circumstances, which is dignified and salvific. The present task is to recover the Hindu context of self-willed death in cases of severe illness and debilitating old age in order to contribute to the Indian debate initiated by Tukol.

Such a challenge that looks to the Indian past makes timely the historical, textual study undertaken here. It may inform the contemporary debate as it unfolds in India and serve as a basis for cross-cultural comparisons when the topic is historical reflections on euthanasia. Such a study will illumine how self-willed death in certain situations of old age and disease was found in India throughout much of history but was eliminated in the early modern period. In comparison, euthanasia in the sense of "freedom to leave" was rarely found in the West after the Graeco-Roman period, although today its merits are increasingly debated as withdrawal of treatment becomes a common phenomenon in hospitals and the debate over compassionate murder continues.

II. Life Affirmation and the Issue of Self-willed Death in the Vedic Period

Prosperity, progeny, and longevity summarize the earliest Weltanschauung of the Aryans in India. Repeatedly in the *Ṛg Veda,* the earliest text, the deities are invoked to shower these benefits on worshippers who perform sacrifice and praise the gods. It is the desire for longevity that interests us here. According to *Ṛg.* III.3.7, for instance, the god Agni is requested to bless the sacrificer with good progeny and long life. Agni is called the universal protector of bodies (*Ṛg.* III.4.2) and is addressed as the source of strength who will give abundant vitality and exemption from sickness and danger (*Ṛg.* III.18.4). The Lord himself is praised as the imperishable life principle (*Ṛg.* III.9.1) and the Aśvins (the physician-gods) are beseeched for good health (*Rg.* I.89.4). The concept of one hundred years represents the ideal of longevity:

> O gods, may we hear with our ears what is beneficial, may we see with our eyes what is good. With firm limbs and sound bodies, having sung your praises, may we reach old age, our minds steadfast on god. May one hundred years await us wherein old age is assured, wherein sons will become fathers. May no harm be done to us in the midst of the course of life.
>
> (*Ṛg.* I.89.8–9. English translation of Geldner 1951, 114)

A preoccupation of the Vedas is long life, perhaps because life was precarious on account of disease and war, and the life span was relatively short. The deities are invoked to protect the body, invigorate it with energy, provide it with sustenance, exempt it from disease, or, if necessary, heal it so that one may live the full term of life which is one hundred years.[8] In that the deities themselves are the imperishable life force, they can take the individual across the difficulties of life. Whether we view the charms described in the *Atharva Veda* as contemporary to or in continuity with the *Ṛg Veda*, prayers for long life and health contained therein reflect the same life affirmation.

> Live thou, thriving a hundred autumns, a hundred winters, and a hundred springs! May Indra, Agni, Savitar, Bṛhaspati (grant) thee a hundred years! I have snatched him (from death) with an oblation that secures a life of a hundred years."
>
> (Bloomfield 1897, 49)

Old age is veritably a blessing from the gods. Prayers for health and protection from disease and other misfortunes indicate that the body is viewed positively. Indeed, so strong is the Vedic life affirmation that immortality is viewed as a continuity to the good, long life, albeit in another realm (*svarga*). Immortality itself is virtually a secondary interest. The perception of a rupture occurs only with the idea that Yama, the god of death, and his messengers may take one away. Both the notion of premature death or relegation to the realm of Yama cast a shadow on happiness and reflect that life is indeed precarious. But, by and large, optimism through confidence in divine protection (and praise, ritual, and charm as human actions to foster the gods' good will) dominates the orientation. If we try to understand this Vedic premise of longevity as a historian of religions, we realize that the concept of longevity, which informs other concepts, is more than an expression of the life principle at the core of human existence, for it is nuanced by salient features of *Ṛg Vedic* society.

Early *Ṛg Vedic* society is an extension of the concept of family and kin, a veritable "being-in-common" where religion and society are not only immersed in each other but also extend beyond the human realm. Accordingly, the collectivity includes (1) all ancestors and (2) all deities who cross over to the human sphere (to which they can communicate by virtue of their anthropomorphism—often on the analogy of an "acquaintance" to the immediate family such as guest, envoy, friend, guide, physician, and so forth—but from which they distinguish themselves by their natural, cosmic, and superhuman traits). Because of the deities' difference from the human collectivity, they are to be treated with respect, deference, and as allies to ensure the maintenance of order (*ṛta*) and well-being, including a long, healthy life surrounded by kin.

It is for this reason that sacrifice was in vogue. Sacrifice is primarily a way to forge a bonding between oneself and the deities, that is, to forge a sacral relationship. Because of this bonding, it is hoped that the deities will protect one through life. The corollary of this statement is that death as a concept of annihilation is marginalized or destroyed on account of the organic view of well-being and the bonding with the deities. The extra antidote is the charm, which magically helps to keep Yama, god of death, away.

Without the natural optimism of a youthful population and the security provided by kinship (the family, tribe, etc.), such an optimistic view of life as one hundred autumns, despite the precariousness of life and the relatively short life span, probably would not have developed. Moreover, there would not have been such confidence at the core of the Aryan migration into India, a confidence in power and dominion so great that for a long time it was not eroded by the many battles with the native inhabitants (not to mention among the Aryan tribes themselves).

With such life affirmation, which is related to the sacramentalization of life but never quite becomes a principle of the sanctity of life, it does not surprise us to find no discussion of suicide (*ātmahatyā, ātmaghāta*) in the *Veda*. And yet, by the 6th century B.C.E., we find clues that suicide is becoming an issue in society at the same time that the categories of *mors voluntaria heroica* and *mors voluntaria religiosa* are emerging. To account for this dramatic change, we must take a closer look at the period under discussion.

In the late *Ṛg Veda* and the literature of the Brāhmaṇas, an interest in control develops. Much of the Vedic energy was consumed by family concerns, the establishment of dominion over the land, and the founding of new Aryan settlements. By the time of the texts of the Brāhmaṇas, there is a desire to control human life, society, and cosmos. More specifically, control is extended in two directions. It is extended over the gods who are now subject to the will of the emerging priests and intelligentsia (the Brahmins who call themselves gods on earth, for they can guarantee the results of the system of sacrifice). Control is also extended over the non-Aryan inhabitants who are gradually integrated into the social order by adjusting the metaphor of organic unity to accommodate the hierarchy imposed by ruler and ruled, hence kingship and the rudimentary caste system.

On initial view, the new concerns with control and system suggest that the passage from kin groups, inclusive of the federation of tribes, to the creation of kingdoms was a relatively peaceful process. But, if we read between the lines of the Brāhmaṇas, complement this source by comparative data from other societies undergoing a transition to kingdoms, and finally deduce certain antecedents from the literature of Jainism and Buddhism, then a different view of this transitional period comes to the foreground. To put matters simply, there are clues that the epoch was fraught with terrible violence:

> However peaceful and harmless the śrauta ritual may look, there can be no doubt about its violent origin in the heroic battle sacrifice epitomizing the warrior phase. Over the whole of the orderly and obsessively regulated vedic ritual there still hangs the dark cloud of a heroically violent world where gods and asuras are for ever fighting each other in endlessly recurring rounds of conflict.
>
> (Heesterman 1984, 125)

It is necessary to understand the escalation of this violence at the time of the rise of kingdoms and the variety of reactions to it in the warriors' milieu in order to appreciate the immediate context of (1) *mors voluntaria heroica,* (2) the development of suicide and nonviolence, and (3) the relationship of these to *mors voluntaria religiosa* and euthanasia (which begin to make their textual appearance by the 6th century B.C.E.). Since this aspect of extreme violence, including human sacrifice, has been underestimated by historians in general and historians of religions in particular—because of their focus on the ritual violence of animal sacrifice to the neglect of political violence—the presence of widespread violence needs to be argued before we can look at related religious phenomena. At the risk of a digression, I wish to propose a scenario that to me makes sense of the data. Let me begin by locating my hermeneutic clue in Eli Sagan's *At the Dawn of Tyranny: the Origins of Individualism, Political Oppression, and the State* (1985).

Sagan's thesis is that a study of societies such as ancient Buganda in Africa and ancient Tonga, Tahiti, and Hawaii in Polynesia reveal the emergence of kingdoms, that is, complex socieites. Complex societies are characterized by the creation of a form of social cohesion other than kinship. This cohesion is the State, which is organized by loyalty to the king and fear of his power to oppress. The State develops a centralized monarchy, organized priesthood, hierarchically ordered social system, rich culture full of imaginative and differentiated cultural forms (such as epic poetry and theatre), and a religious orientation based on a sacrificial complex. In the State, it is common to find royal incest, prostitution, adultery games, sexual exhibitionism, and compulsive gambling. It is striking, says Sagan, that human sacrifice is a characteristic form of ritual aggression during the rise of kingdoms and tyranny is rampant.

Leaving aside Sagan's larger thesis of cultural evolution with its psychoanalytic moorings, it may be argued that his analysis of complex society, involving the transition from chieftainship to simple kingdoms, resonates well with the period of Indian history from the time of the Brāhmaṇas to the emergent epic of the *Mahābhārata*. In India, one finds not only the transition from tribe to kingdom but also the development of social hierarchy in the form of caste, a well-defined priesthood (which collaborates with the State), the advent of epic poetry, theatre, a religious complex based on sacrifice, cases of royal incest, prostitution, adultery, sexual exhibitionism, and gambling. In fact, Sagan's diagnostic features of early kingdoms is a good characterization of this period in India.[9]

When hierarchy is abused, argues Sagan (1985), tyranny is born. Moreover, "license is implicit in omnipotence;" "the two great licenses are the sexual and the aggressive, and early kings were expected to exercise both" (320). With reference to the latter, "a king was a king because he could kill at will" (321), even though he could also be the benevolent protector of the land. The prevalence of sacrifice in complex societies testifies both to aggression and to an attempt to be omnipotent by controlling life and death. The latter is symbolized par excellence by human sacrifice. If this hermeneutical clue from Sagan is correct, then one should expect to find human sacrifice in the Brāhmaṇas. The texts, in fact, point to this reality. A parallel to the horse sacrifice is the human sacrifice. One text (see Keith 1925, 347ff) mentions the offering of 166 men at 11 posts. Keith attributes this to priestly imagination, because there is lack of detail. But the account should be taken more seriously, given comparative evidence[10] and the possibility of later Brahmanical editing of the texts (in the face of Buddhist and Jaina critiques) to eliminate details of human sacrifice or to make them symbolic (as in the *Śatapatha*, *Taittirīya*, and the *Sūtras*).

Keith tells us that the king, on this occasion, may give up his goods and enter into the life of a wandering mendicant. The meaning escapes Keith, as it does more recent scholars who view the violence inclusive of human sacrifice only as a survival from the very distant past. This ritual was performed initially in order to achieve human success, magically, as it were, by taking a human victim. The later context for this ritual ensures a regular succession to the throne by having the king remove himself from the seat of government, give up his power, and withdraw to the forest. The performance of the human sacrifice on this occasion no doubt is to symbolize the king's sacrifice of himself for the sake of his son. The son, in turn, will perform rituals at the time of his father's death to secure heaven for his father.

Keith suggests that there are two doctrines in the Brāhmaṇas that prefigure approval of religious, self-willed death from religious motives: (1) the proper sacrifice is that of a man's self, and (2) the final act of the *pur-*

uṣamedha and *sarvamedha* is "the giving away by the performer of the whole of his possessions, including in the latter case even the land, and his wandering into the forest, doubtless as a preliminary to an early death" (1922, 34).

These doctrines must be appreciated, as has been suggested, in the context of the rise of kingdoms, which led to a particularly violent phase of Indian history when the sacrifice of animals was rampant and that of humans not unknown. Before we can understand fully the meaning of this human sacrifice by and of the king, we need to look more closely at the concept of heroic death and a variety of reactions to violence in the Kṣatriya milieu.

Death in battle has been rewarded by most cultures, for there must be some compensation for male risk in battle beyond immediate material gain. Thus *Ṛg Veda* X.154.3 (*Atharva* 18.2.17), which may be dated to about the same period as the Brāhmaṇas and the rise of kingdoms in the Gangetic plain, suggests "that warriors losing life in battle reap the same rewards that those who make gifts of a thousand cows in sacrifices secure" (Kane 1973, 58). Later texts indicate that death in battle is equated to participation in the Brahmanical sacrifice itself. "*Śāntiparva* 78.31 states that just as those who join in the bath of the king at the end of the Aśvamedha sacrifice are purified of all sins, so all soldiers (of whatever caste and on whatever side) killed in battle become pure by the destruction of their sins" (Kane III, 1973, 58). Texts such as *Gītā* II.31–37; *Manu* VII. 87–89; *Yāj.* I. 324, and so on make the reward explicitly heaven.

Warriors who were defeated in battle sometimes killed themselves out of shame or killed themselves rather than be captured. Similarly, women escaped capture, rape, and slavery—at the time of defeat or after their husbands were killed in battle or when they killed themselves—by willing their own death. With great violence in society, we can predict a high level of violence against women. As Sagan says, the power to take a woman away from another man is a double tyranny (1985, 291), that is, it is an act of aggression against the woman and the man. These forms of self-willed death no doubt were also associated with heaven.

If attainment of heaven was guaranteed by heroic death in battle or self-willed death to escape capture, rape, and slavery (an idea which may well date from the period of the Brāhmaṇas, though it is explicitly found in later texts), then, according to this cultural logic, warriors who did not die in or because of battle, despite a valiant career, were not rewarded. (Even *Bhīṣmaparva* 17.11 states that "it is a sinful act for a kṣatriya to die in his house from some disease; the ancient code of conduct for him is that he should meet death from steel" (Kane 1973, 3:58; see also *Śalyaparva* 5.32, *Śānti* 97.23 and 25). We may surmise that this insistence on death in battle would seem unjust to those old warriors who had risked their lives on numerous occasions in battle, yet survived. May we not assume that such survivors extended the cultural logic to include heroic self-sacrifice toward the end of life to ensure that they too attained heaven? Furthermore, it is likely that the close association of *mors voluntaria heroica* toward the end of life (as a substitute for death in battle) leading to the attainment of heaven or deification, in turn, posited the seeds for the general connection of self-willed death and the religious goal, heaven or enlightenment, in the emergent religions of the Gangetic plain, hence the phenomenon of *mors voluntaria religiosa.*

Besides this concept of heroic death to ensure heaven, self-willed death no doubt was also viewed as an appropriation of the violence of the king. We recall that the king in early complex society is autonomous and can do virtually anything that he wants, even to the extent of killing others as sacrificial victims. We have also indicated that the king's male kin or other warriors in the society may be jealous of his power and wish to imitate it, yet be afraid of royal reprisal should they go about killing whom they please when they please. It is conceivable that some warriors may imitate the king and his omnipotence by killing themselves, especially since we know from modern psychology that the thing and its opposite may be identical in the unconscious. The violence of the king that makes him omnipotent, in that he decides who lives and who dies, is achieved by others who develop complete power over the self to the point of killing the self and thereby achieving power over life and death. Just as the king becomes a destroyer and takes a human victim to ward off magically his own destruction and to achieve success, so too a warrior may desire to imitate the king's omnipotence and to ward off his own destruction by taking himself as victim. In this light, violence directed outward and violence directed inward are intimately related. Jealousy, anger, or fear of the king's power, which may involve a desire to kill him, is deflected back on the warriors who kill themselves instead, thereby becoming omnipotent through taking themselves as sacrificial victims. Could it not be, then, that the category of *mors voluntaria religiosa* was directly connected to the warriors' milieu, almost as an interiorization of the heroic idiom and heroic *mors voluntaria* of the day.[11]

One common form of self-willed death became death by fire, for the Vedic sacrificial cult was focused on fire, understood as the god Agni. A sacrifice may have a specific purpose: to obtain something by giving something up. So also voluntary, self-willed death became linked to a specific purpose: to obtain freedom (heaven or liberation) through an act of omnipotence, involving the sacrifice of the self. In that self-inflicted, human sacrifice gave one omnipotence and the power over life itself, this negative power, as it were, could lead to the idea of liberation from violence. Once again, we discover antecedents to *mors voluntaria religiosa*. The extreme violence of the age provoked other reactions as well. One was nonviolence. When a more nonviolent self-sacrifice (such as fasting to death) was substituted for violent self-sacrifice, the goal remained the same. But for some, the more nonviolent means no doubt seemed superior, either as a way to escape violence or as a protest to violence (albeit still by killing the self, nonviolently, as it were). If omnipotence through self-sacrifice was related to asceticism and withdrawal to the forest, as nonviolent ways to escape the materialism and violence of the age, then such escapism was no longer a cowardly act, anathema to a warrior. Rather, it was positively appropriated and converted into a religious path and goal epitomized by nonviolence and a fast to death, which ensured heaven or liberation. Such an equation eventually was recorded in the texts. According to Kane (1973, 3:58), "Two men pierce the orb of the sun (i.e. reach heavenly worlds), viz. an ascetic endowed with Yoga and a soldier killed with facing the enemy" (*Parāśara* 3.37).

In this way, violence and nonviolence were intimately related, in that nonviolence was to be substituted for violence to achieve the goal of omnipotence. Killing the self may have taken more courage and heroism than aggression directed outward. The feeling of omnipotence may have been even greater than that of the king and may have given rise to the idea of the superiority of the ascetic who wills his or her own death. If voluntary self-willed death had its seeds in the warriors' milieu, its significance as a method for omnipotence no doubt was noted by others in the society, especially the Brahmins who were sensitive to issues of power in their competition with the Kṣatriyas. In the Āraṇyakas or the Forest Treatises, the sequel to the Brāhmaṇas, we find both Kṣatriyas and Brahmins withdrawing to the forest to practise asceticism. To the extent that the new ascetic power did not threaten the king's power, he allowed its expression. But the ascetic's power and the king's power were bound to conflict, unless models for their complementarity were developed.

Now we are in a position to understand why the king not only sacrificed others to symbolize his omnipotence but also withdrew to the forest to practise asceticism, possibly leading to some form of self-willed death. As a warrior, he probably wished to secure heaven since he did not die in battle. As the most powerful person, his form of death had to be at least equivalent to other Kṣatriyas, who had discovered the key to heaven and immortality through self-willed death. This analysis is not to underestimate the sociological side of the phenomenon: the king's abandonment of power and physical withdrawal also eased the problem of the transfer of power in the royal family.

While such equivalences and substitutions surrounding the issue of self-willed death no doubt appealed to the Kṣatriyas and some Brahmins, they must have appeared as forms of suicide to those Brahmins who supported the Vedic prescription of the natural life span. It should not surprise us, then, to find that prohibitions against suicide start to appear in the subsequent texts, the Upaniṣads. It also should not surprise us to find that the Upaniṣads reflect philosophical ferment, as thinkers try to come to terms with changing values and the new religious perspectives developed by Buddhism and Jainism. The issue of the natural life span or self-willed death will be focal to the new thinking that tries to reconcile violence and nonviolence, materialism and asceticism, and action and withdrawal.

To conclude, the rise of kingdoms, which resulted in great violence including human sacrifice, was the background for the emergence of *mors voluntaria heroica, mors voluntaria religiosa,* suicide, and nonviolence through a number of equivalences and substitutions. These developments played no small part in transforming the Vedic world view, as we shall see in the next section.

III. The Upaniṣadic Weltanschauung and Adjustment of the Vedic Value of Longevity

Central to the Upaniṣadic transformation was the Brahmanical reaction to, if not participation in, the polarizations of the times. Brahmins, we must not forget, were the priests who consecrated and supported the new kings by their sacrificial expertise. They were not far removed from the seat of power and the violence of the age, for the religious microcosm involved sacrifice. At the same time, Brahmins also vied with Kṣatriyas for power, albeit defined ritualistically and intellectually. As asceticism became a new means to achieve power, it is conceivable that more and more Brahmins appropriated this new idiom for omnipotence. By making themselves equal to the king, they not only elevated themselves but also brought the king lower. Indeed, in the Upaniṣads Brahmins often learned the secret truth of this "ascetic" omnipotence from the Kṣatriyas, but they claimed that Brahmins were at the head of the hierarchy. In short, the individualism of the age was not without its power struggles.

The new Weltanschauung presented in the Upaniṣads, which reflects integration of the challenges of the epoch, is based on a polarity between this–worldly suffering through death after death (*punarmṛtyu*), later understood as birth after birth (the wheel of *saṁsāra*) and the bliss of liberation (*mokṣa*), which transcends the human condition altogether. The rupture in existence is no longer the rupture of death caused by Yama, though this idea lingers. It is the rupture caused by the soul's disengagement from matter, nature, and body alike. This rupture is now viewed as categorically positive. Human life is no longer valued in its own right, more precisely, for the sake of progeny, family, and material well-being so central to Aryan identity in the *Ṛg Veda*. Rather, it is viewed from two competing perspectives: human life as necessary for salvation, and the body as the cause of bondage. While the new theory of rebirth posits that the individual may have had or may have in the future other kinds of birth (for example, as an animal), it is only in a human birth that an individual may seek enlightenment. Hence, the value of human life is defined positively by the unique opportunity that it provides for the pursuit of salvation. Human status is a product of an individual's *karma*, a result of good actions in previous lives. Abuse of this human status is productive of bad *karma*. The result may be loss of human status in the next life and with it opportunity for salvation, thus perpetuating the "bondage of rebirth (*saṃsāra*). At the same time, human status is viewed negatively, for the body is the expression of bondage and suffering. Thus, the meaning of human existence has shifted to instrumentality, that is, human embodiment as a means to obtain the supreme goal. The corollary of this shift is the opposition of soul and body and a stress on individual responsibility for salvation. One can cheat Death of its prey through yoga, comprising austerities and knowledge. This leads to real transcendence and immortality, understood as attaining the Absolute (*brahman*) and the True Self (*ātman*). As Blackburn notes (1985, 255), "Vedic sacrifices were designed to ward off death temporarily and attain a full life span for men. A more total conquest of death was the goal in the philosophies of the Upanishads, Buddhism, and Jainism."

The Upaniṣads, considered the end or culmination of the Veda, present this new view of human existence, though the older Vedic perspective is generally incorporated. For example, in *Chāndogya Upaniṣad* 11.2 the Gāyatrī chant (which reflects the Vedic orientation) and the breaths of the yogi (which reflect the Upaniṣadic view) together ensure a long, prosperous life (the old Vedic ideal).

In *Kauśītaki Upaniṣad* 4.8, it is said that the (Upaniṣadic) Brahman fulfills the Vedic goals of life such as longevity. When Brahman in the self is reverenced as the breath of life (*asu*), one "does not die before the time" (*Kauśītaki* 4.13). Accordingly, the appreciation of longevity, which is related to the sacramentalization of life, is often integrated into the Upaniṣadic perspective. While the Vedas relate longevity to vitality and, in the final analysis, animation or breath itself, the Upaniṣads see breath as a symbol of the soul (*ātman*) and immortality. Long life, moreover, is still desired, but there appears a basic disjunction between *saṃsāra* and *mokṣa*. Yoga as a magic power sometimes replaces praise, sacrifice, and charm as the protector and preserver of life and ultimately the conqueror of death. Pursuit of yoga, however, may be relegated to the last stage of life. Here, too, a long healthy life is necessary to ensure that there is sufficient time for the pursuit of yoga culminating in enlightenment. Through yoga, one conquers sickness, old age, and also death (*Śvetāśvatara*. 2.12).

The Upaniṣadic view, however, poses a tension between the Vedic view of a life span of one hundred years and the idea that action (*karma*) creates bondage. To overcome this conundrum, it is argued that although the renouncer may desire to live a hundred years, *karma* will not bind him after he has achieved liberation.

> Even while doing deeds here,
> One may desire to live a hundred years.
> Thus on thee—not otherwise than this is it—
> The deed (*karman*) adheres not on the man.
>
> (*Īśa* 2; Hume 1968, 362)

While the Vedic life affirmation is incorporated into the Upaniṣadic Weltanschauung, so that yoga is like a magical power which both protects life to full term and leads to liberation, a new negative view of old age is also found: "May I, who am the glory of the glories, not go to hoary and toothless, yea to toothless and hoary and driveling [old age]! Yea, may I not go to driveling [old age!]" (*Chāndogya* 8.14; Hume 1968, 273). This verse expresses a desire to avoid extreme debilitating old age, which may be a reflection of the fact that the life span is increasing.

Despite ambivalence over human life and the body, the Vedic respect for longevity and the natural life span remains the dominant Brahmanical attitude. This may be the reason for the following verse, which may be taken as condemning suicide, especially if suicide as a form of escape from violence is becoming common in society.

> Devilish (*asurya*) are those worlds called,
> With blind darkness (*tamas*) covered o'er!
> Unto them, on deceasing, go
> Whatever folk are slayers of the Self.
>
> (*Īśa* 3; Hume 1968, 362)[12]

But another interpretation of this verse is that it alludes to the growing custom of self-willed death by the warrior folk "who are slayers of the self."

To highlight the distinctively Brahmanical/Hindu response to the challenges of the 6th century B.C.E., it is important to consider briefly the Jaina and Buddhist views that draw from the same ascetic and intellectual currents and which, in turn, prompt some of the Brahmanical rethinking that appears in the Upaniṣads. The first observation is that Jainism and Buddhism share the premise of *saṁsāra* and liberation. *Saṁsāra* is bondage, and bondage is suffering, while, once again, enlightenment is transcendence of the human condition.

As an early ascetic movement, Jainism makes a categorical imperative out of nonviolence; the idea takes on moralistic overtones. And yet, the Jaina idea of liberation as radical autonomy (*kaivalya*) and the custom of fasting to death (*sallekhanā*) remain close to the ideas of 1) asceticism as withdrawal from violence, and 2) omnipotence as the ability to kill the self. Indeed, Jainism is the first religion to formalize and legitimate the practise of *mors voluntaria heroica*—which, as we have argued, was in vogue in the warrior and ascetic circles—as a kind of *mors voluntaria religiosa*. Jainism also seems to be the first Indian religion to associate *mors voluntaria religiosa* with euthanasia as a form of self-willed death at the time of debilitating old age or severe illness.

The practise of *sallekhanā* is described in the *Ācārāṅga*. It is said that the wise one should know that the time for death has come. If one falls sick in the midst of the fast, one should take food until well. One should not long for life or death. One should die by the elimination of food (*bhaktapratyākhyānamaraṇa*). One should lie on the ground, rejoice in pain, and, even if animals feed on one's flesh, one should not kill them, nor stir from the position (*Ācārāṅga* I.7.8.1–10; Jacobi 1884, 74–76).

What is striking about the early Jaina perspective is not only that asceticism and mortification of the flesh have been taken to their ultimate conclusion. It is also that a religion which has, as a cardinal doctrine, *ahiṁsā* or non-injury to any living creature—including never killing an insect intentionally or unintentionally—yet has as an ideal: religious, self-willed death. The rationale is that the virtually liberated person is beyond the opposition of life and death. The body will be eliminated anyway when the *karmas* are used up. A cognizance of imminent death together with perfect control and a peaceful means, which is gradual and mindful, is veritably the good death. That the almost enlightened one maintains *ahiṁsā* or non-injury to the very end and does not harm insects or wild animals that eat away the flesh is considered a fulfillment of the religious code. Such was the attempt to reconcile the apparent contradiction between self-willed death and *ahiṁsā* given the internal logic of the religion. Thus, it may be argued that Jainism tried to harness the power of violent death through yogic control and fasting as a means to conquer totally death and *saṁsāra*.

More specifically, fasting to death (*sallekhanā*) was given a religious meaning by understanding it to be the means of removing those *karmas* that remain even after ascetic purification, especially those that define the existence of the body itself or bondage. *Sallekhanā* was to be done in a religious framework by monks and nuns and was to be controlled by a number of constraints, such as years of preparatory purification, meditation leading to true knowledge, and timing toward the end of life. By associating the fast to death with salvation and governing the practise through certain constraints, *sallekhanā* was distinguished from both *mors voluntaria heroica* and suicide proper.

The purpose of *sallekhanā* was ostensibly to eliminate the body for the purpose of eliminating bondage toward the end of the natural life span. Some monastics resorted to the practise earlier in life when faced by a seemingly incurable disease, even though the merits of doing so were debated in the early tradition. It was thought that the sick could not sustain the austerities involved in the controlled elimination of food.

Buddhism, too, had its roots in a reaction to the violence of the day. Buddha, who grew up among his own kin (the *Śakyas*)—whose tribal territory was on the periphery of the Gangetic plain, which witnessed the rise of kingdoms—was shocked when he first encountered the political violence by the Kṣatriyas and the sacrificial violence by the Brahmins of the plains. Like the Jainas, Buddha gave a moralistic interpretation to nonviolence but was careful to seek a Middle Path and to avoid the polarizations of the times. It was Buddha, in particular, who promoted his message by castigating the sacrificial system of Brahmins. Moreover, he continually sought ways to solve disputes nonviolently and to encourage warriors to lay down their arms and take up occupations that would not involve killing (Sinha 1986, 25–26).

Buddha condemns suicide (or self-willed death?) in no uncertain terms. In the *Pārājika*, Buddha says: "A monk who preaches suicide, who tells man: 'Do away with this wretched life, full of suffering and sin; death is better,' in fact preaches murder, is a murderer, is no longer a monk" (De La Vallée Poussin 1922, 125). Because this remark is addressed to monks, we conclude that Buddha also excludes any form of religious, self-willed death and warns against pessimism even in the midst of the religious path. Since one of Buddha's five precepts is not to kill any living thing (*ahiṁsā*), the prohibition on suicide follows logically. Similarly, the idea of self-willed death at the time when one's end is near is discouraged, if not prohibited outright. Buddha, on the contrary, encourages individuals to seek enlightenment as early as possible. If suffering becomes overwhelming, one may not be able to have the right mindfulness so necessary to realize the Four Noble Truths.

And yet it seems that meditation on suffering did make some disciples of Buddha pessimistic and led them to the point of suicide. This may be a reflection of the considerable pessimism existent in the society at large, which was related to the violence and turbulent changes brought about by the formation of the kingdoms. Yet, enlightenment as conceived by Buddha was no easy affair, and the quest could engender deep despair if wisdom were not forthcoming. There are three stories of aspirants who are about to commit suicide, so frustrated are they by their inability to progress spiritually,[13] and one story of a monk who contemplates suicide because he is suffering from a terrible illness.

In the first three cases, if despair over the difficulty of realizing enlightenment (*nibbāna*) prompts preparation for suicide, thoughts of suicide in turn, prompt realization. It is the story that recounts how a monk contemplates suicide because he is suffering from severe illness, which interests us here.

In *Saṁyutta* iii. 123, it is told how Vakkali, who is ill and suffering great pain, is comforted by Buddha. Buddha tells him that his death will be auspicious. Then the monk utters one final time the profession of faith and kills himself by the sword. It is hard to think that Buddha condoned this act from our previous discussion of the early Buddhist perspective, but he must have considered this case an exception (given his compassion and the severity of the disease). Even though Buddha considered the experience of suffering as potentially redemptive, he was known as a good physician. Perhaps because of this pragmatic orientation, he was willing to entertain euthanasia in exceptional circumstances. His position on euthanasia was also made possible because life has instrumental value in his teachings; he did not have to worry about the sanctity of life. Moreover, it is possible to make sense of the various early Buddhist discussions if we understand that the desire of Buddha is to prevent any form of self-willed death (whether prompted by escapism or by religious motives) precisely because various kinds of self-willed death were becoming prevalent in society. It is likely that he viewed self-willed death as a kind of extremism and preferred to substitute meditation on death as the means to achieve omniscience and omnipotence. Such a position, however, does not preclude the possibility of Buddha's compassion toward one who is extremely ill and wishes to die. At the same time, many of Buddha's unenlightened disciples may have viewed the issue differently. Most of them were warriors (Kṣatriyas). If heroic, self-willed death were indeed common in society, then it should not surprise us to find that some of Buddha's followers take up the sword out of frustration, escapism, or as a substitute for death in battle. Whatever the motivation, these close encounters with suicide (or self-willed death) are described in a didactic way in the Pāli Canon to show how sudden realization may occur at the moment of total despair.

To conclude, we find that a new Weltanschauung emerged by the 6th century B.C.E., the premises of which were shared by Hinduism, Buddhism, and Jainism. These three religions all had to come to terms with such deep polarizations as materialism and asceticism and violence and nonviolence, which developed with the massive upheavals in the society caused by the rise of kingdoms or complex society. Moreover, the three religions all tried to tame the violence. Their common concern to prohibit suicide suggests that suicide was becoming a problem in society, perhaps because pessimism and escapism were spreading among the populace at large in this age of great violence, especially if the warriors promoted a form of self-willed death. The response of the three religions to *mors voluntaria heroica,* however, differed. While Brahmins recognized heroic, self-willed death as a prevalent Kṣatriya or warrior practise, which was extending into ascetic circles, Brahmins did not wish to see the practise move beyond the Kṣatriyas circle. Most Brahmins continued to insist on the old Vedic ideal of longevity, "one hundred autumns," even when liberation occurred earlier in life and only the continued existence of the body defined bondage. Jainism, by contrast, highlighted the religious dimension of *mors voluntaria heroica* so that it is more proper to speak of a *mors voluntaria religiosa* in the form of a fast to death by ascetics, which brought the salvific dimension to the foreground. Because this fast to death was distinguished from suicide by a number of constraints, it was viewed as a legitimate and preferred option for monastics toward the end of their life. Buddhism, differed from Jainism by not endorsing self-willed death for monastics. In this sense, Buddhism was more like Brahmanism in its insistence on the natural life span and meditation as the way to eliminate bondage. Buddhism, however, focused more on suffering than did Brahmanism, which clung to the old life affirmation of the Vedas despite the growing pessimism. While all three religions remained sensitive to the issue of the natural life span and reacted to any premature escapism, they also all created scope for the practise of euthanasia. Brahmins came to endorse the idea of withdrawing to the forest toward the end of life, which may have put them in contact with the practise of self-willed death. (We recall that already in the *Śatapatha Brāhmaṇa* the king withdrew to the forest to facilitate the problem of succession, possibly with a view to an early—and self-willed—death.) When severe disease set in, it was but a small step to will death, having already renounced both possessions and relations. Jainism recognized, although it did not encourage, the practise of *sallekhanā* or the fast to death when severe illness occurred. And Buddha himself, through his compassion for the extreme suffering of Vakkali, condoned his self-willed death in these exceptional circumstances.

In short, all three religions had to come to terms with the transformation of the sacramental view of human life to an instrumental view where life continued to have fundamental value but not intrinsic value. We noticed that this instrumental view of human life may be correlated with a concern with suicide and the practise of heroic *mors voluntaria.* This new orientation meant that certain questions regarding the quality of life could be raised. This allowed issues of euthanasia to be considered, for euthanasia is related to the quality of life when one is very ill or old. Each of the religions adjusted to the practise of *mors voluntaria* with sensitivity to the idea of the natural life span, despite the differences of approach to self-willed death from acceptance within certain constraints to denial of the practise. Whatever the differences, greater sympathy was given by all three religions to situations that involved debilitating old age and apparent terminal illness. Finally, the discussion of *mors voluntaria heroica* and *mors voluntaria religiosa* proceeded hand in hand with discussions of suicide as killing the self and *ahiṁsā* as not killing any sentient thing. The Jainas made *ahiṁsā* a tenet of their religion but also accepted *sallekhanā*. Consequently, they had to argue why *sallekhanā* is not killing the self by resorting to the idea of a peaceful mode and religious context, which was confined to advanced mendicants. Buddhists also accepted the principle of *ahiṁsā* but substituted meditation on death for actual self-willed death. While there was an attempt to encourage non-monastics to be nonviolent, a difference of ethics between monastics and the laity was permitted. This avoided the problem posed by insisting on universal nonviolence (*ahiṁsā*) in the Kṣatriya milieu. Brahmins were faced with the difficulty of adjusting to the new situation through elimination, or harmonization of, the sacrificial system (which involved killing) and *ahiṁsā*. Brahmins had sacramentalized the elderly king's withdrawal to the forest, which involved human sacrifice and may have led the king to self-sacrifice in the sense of *mors voluntaria heroica*. They also began to voice concern regarding suicide. In the next period, Brahmins will try to reconcile acceptance of *mors voluntaria*, prohibition of suicide, and *ahiṁsā* either by a multiple ethic,[14] involving different rules for different groups or situations, or by arguing how euthanasia is an exception to the general rule. Moreover, in the after centuries, *mors voluntaria religiosa*—which was probably first legitimated by Jainism—spreads to Brahmanism/Hinduism, takes root in Buddhism, and also extends to the laity in Jainism. While there are debates regarding the legitimacy of the practise, there is still accord when the context is terminal illness and debilitating old age.

IV. Religious, Self-Willed Death in the Hindu *Smṛti* Texts Compared with Similar Developments in Buddhism and Jainism

Contained in the Hindu *smṛti* texts (6th century B.C.E. to 10th century C.E.) are a number of injunctions and prohibitions that provide guidelines for proper conduct, as well as document changing attitudes in society. With reference to our topic of concern, we find that suicide is severely condemned throughout this period. It is worth quoting Kane's summary of the *smṛti* statements on suicide (*ātmaghāta* or *ātmahatyā*) understood as self-destruction usually prompted by extreme emotion, depression, or some external circumstance over which the individual thinks he/she has no control.

> The Dharmaśāstra writers generally condemn suicide or an attempt to commit suicide as a great sin. Parāśara (IV. 1–2) states that if a man or woman hangs himself or herself through extreme pride or extreme rage or through affliction or fear, he or she falls into hell for sixty thousand years. Manu V.89 says that no water is to be offered for the benefit of the souls of those who kill themselves. The Ādiparva (179.20) declares that one who commits suicide does not reach blissful worlds. Vas. Dh. S. (23.14–16) ordains "whoever kills himself becomes *abiśasta* (guilty of mortal sin) and his *sapiṇḍas* have to perform no death rites for him; a man becomes a killer of the self when he destroys himself by wood (i.e. by fire), water, clods and stones (i.e. by striking his head against a stone), weapon, poison, or ropes (i.e. by hanging)." They also quote a verse "that [a] *dvija* who through affection performs the last rites of a man who commits suicide must undergo the penance of Cāndrāyaṇa with Taptakṛcchra". Vas.Dh.S. 23.18 prescribes that when a person tries to do away with himself by such methods as hanging, if he dies, his body should be smeared with impure things and if he lives he should be fined two hundred *paṇas;* his friends and sons should each be fined one *paṇa* and then they should undergo the penance laid down in the śāstra.
>
> (Kane 1974, 2:924)

This discussion suggests that the phenomenon of suicide is now common in the society. Indeed, if the *Mahābhārata* is any indication, there is yet polarization. Violence is prevalent (in fact, the *Mahābhārata* continues to fit Sagan's paradigm of complex society) and so is the desire to withdraw from society (in the *Gītā*, Arjuna desires to withdraw from battle and renounce action). Perhaps there is even greater despair in the society at this time, for warriors such as Arjuna question the very purpose of being a Kṣatriya.

The *locus classicus* for the desire to commit suicide is the example of old King Dhṛtharāṣṭra in the epic *Mahābhārata* (*Strīparva*). Dhṛtarāṣṭra, overcome by grief as he faces the carnage of the great war and the slaughter of his kin (including his own sons), weeps uncontrollably, falls on the ground, laments, and resolves to go the long way that leads to the realm of Brahmā. In other words, he wishes to die by the great journey (*mahāprasthāna*), which involves wandering until he drops dead and goes to heaven. Knowing that it is self-indulgence arising from extreme sorrow that has provoked the king to escape his trials by suicide, Vaiśampāyana rebukes such self-pity and lectures him sternly on the meaning of death.[15] In the arguments to dissuade Dhṛtarāṣṭra from committing suicide, we find an endorsement of and appeal to the Kṣatriya's duty. Kṣatriyas are to fight, for warriors who die in battle win fame and heaven. It is important to note that such death is described as a quicker and therefore easier means to heaven than sacrifices, gifts, asceticism, or knowledge. It is as if a Brahmin author were attempting not only to discourage suicide but also to woo Kṣatriyas back from Buddhism and Jainism by appealing to Kṣatriya pride and stressing the idea that heroic death ensures heaven (the Sanskrit texts in the classical period make heaven the explicit goal of death in battle). The Brahmin authors go one step further and claim that death in battle, in fact, is an *easy* way to attain heaven. The dialectic between Brahmins and the heterodox religions was in the making. Attracting the warriors back into the Brahmanical view of the State by discouraging asceticism, suicide (and self-willed death?), and by promoting a philosophy of action was a major task.

While the definition of suicide seems to be all-embracing (any death as the consequence of one's own action), some Brahmin lawgivers, as well as the author(s) of the epics, make exceptions.

> But Atri (218–219) states some exceptions viz. "if one who is very old (beyond 70), one who cannot observe the rules of bodily purification (owing to extreme weakness . . .), one who is so ill that no medical help can be given, kills himself by throwing himself from a precipice or into a fire or water or by fasting, mourning should be observed for him for three days and śrāddha may be performed for him". Aparārka (p. 536) quotes texts of Brahmagarbha, Vivasvat and Gārgya about an householder "he who is suffering from serious illness cannot live, or who is very old, who has no desire left for the pleasures of any of the senses and who has carried out his tasks, may bring about his death at pleasure by resorting to mahāprasthāna, by entering fire or water or by falling from a precipice. By so doing he incurs no sin and his death is far better than *tapas*, and one should not desire to live vainly (without being able to perform the duties laid down by the śāstra)."
>
> (Kane 1974, 2:926)

Clearly here, Brahmin authors accept, in no uncertain terms, the practise of euthanasia (if we understand the premodern meaning of euthanasia to be a good death that is self-willed and self-accomplished as a way to deal with the problems of extreme old age and severe illness).

Modern Western supporters of euthanasia argue that euthanasia should be allowed when one is no longer able to live with dignity and comfort and when the quality of life is intolerably undermined. Brahmin jurists have also sought to define biological, psychological, and social limits for the phenomenon. This was necessitated by the considerable overlap between the desire to escape the difficulties of extreme illness and old age and the desire to commit suicide proper. For, not only are they both forms of self-willed death, they also may be prompted by extreme emotion, depression, or uncontrollable circumstance.

To distinguish euthanasia from suicide, Brahmin jurists proposed a number of constraints. For example, either the illness cannot be treated and death is imminent or the condition of the aged person is such that there is no desire for pleasure. Because all social duties are finished, it is natural to withdraw from life. (In the terminology of modern gerontology, this would be a case of disengagement.) Brahmin authors of the legal texts also give a religious dimension to the context of euthanasia, which helps to distinguish it from suicide. Euthanasia may be done when a person no longer can perform the rites of bodily purification, which may occur in the case of extreme illness or extreme old age. We can understand the Brahmanical position better by looking to the ritual logic of Mīmāṁsā, which is implicit in the formulation of the Brahmanical position. Because these duties are *dharmic* and required, the nonperformance of them, according to the ritual logic of Mīmāṁsā, would ordinarily create demerit/sin (*pāpa*). Since the incapacitated person cannot perform mandatory, religious duties because of circumstances beyond control, it was necessary to create an exception to the general rule regarding required acts. Nonperformance of obligatory action by an incapacitated person is to be considered *dharmic*. If nonperformance of obligatory rituals is considered *dharmic* for an incapacitated person, then euthanasia, which is defined, in part, by the situation of incapacitation, may also be considered *dharmic*. If euthanasia is *dharmic*, then, in Brahmanical terms, it is righteous and religious. Finally, if euthanasia is *dharmic* and therefore religious, it belongs to the category of *mors voluntaria religiosa* and is definitively different from suicide. Such is the legalistic logic. It is important to note that once the jurists create legal scope for euthanasia, they allow easy means, such as jumping from a precipice or into fire and water, unlike Jainas, whose method of fasting to death is more arduous.

It is difficult to know whether the Brahmanical legitimation of euthanasia was a departure from an earlier Brahmanical reluctance to endorse any form of self-willed death, given the prescription of living the natural life span, or whether euthanasia was occasionally practised among Brahmins themselves. What is important is that once, Brahmin jurists reflected on the issue, almost all agreed that it could be condoned in special circumstances for any individual, Brahmins included.

One implication of this legal scope for euthanasia is that responsibility for self-willed death rests ostensibly with the individual. The Law of Karma is the key to understanding the issue of individual responsibility. It is important for an individual to consider the various criteria for euthanasia and to determine whether the desire to die is legitimately a case of euthanasia or whether it is a case of suicide. The distinction is crucial, for the latter generates demerit or sin (*pāpa*) and leads to hell. While an individual was responsible to determine whether the desire to die is legitimate or not (perhaps by remembering the arguments made to convince Dhṛtarāṣṭra to live), the leaders of society were responsible for the larger issue of whether any kind of *mors voluntaria religiosa* should be legitimated. The decision was made on the basis of the scriptures, the practise of the good people, and societal conditions. There was a recognition of how human lives interconnected to determine the social order. One definition of *dharma* was, in fact, social order. Practises such as euthanasia were viewed critically in social terms so that the welfare of society was taken into consideration. Once this had been determined, then an individual was free to choose actions that may be optional but must be *dharmic,* in that they contribute to the general good of society or at least do not obstruct it.

During the classical period under consideration, when much of the *smṛti* literature is composed, two additional considerations arise for Brahmins reflecting on issues such as euthanasia: the principle of *ahiṁsā* or non-injury to any living thing, and the concept of *saṁkalpa* or intention. Let us first consider the principle of *ahiṁsā* (non-injury), which is accepted by Brahmins in this period for their own code of conduct—no doubt as a reaction to criticisms made against them with reference to their earlier endorsement of violence, especially sacrificial violence. Once Brahmins accept *ahiṁsā*, then how can they consider euthanasia to be dharmic when it involves killing the self and killing the self is an obvious denial of the principle of non-injury? As Arvind Sharma has argued in his article "The Religious Justification of War in Hinduism" (*ARC*, 1986), the pursuit and protection of *dharma* provides the religious justification of war. Whereas non-injury to living beings was a *sādhāraṇa-dharma* (duty which applies to all human beings irrespective of stage and station or caste in life), Kṣatriyas had protection of *dharma* also as the special duty of their caste, a duty which belonged to the category of *varṇāśrama-dharma* (duty according to caste and stage of life). According to Sharma, in case of conflict between *varṇāśrama-dharma* and *sādhāraṇa-dharma* (as in the case of the Kṣatriyas), *varṇāśrama-dharma*—which includes both defensive and aggressive warfare when *dharma* is obstructed—generally had precedence in Hinduism.

Since we have found one situation where killing is dharmic, we may assume that the same logic was operant in the Brahmanical understanding of euthanasia. Accordingly, euthanasia as self-willed death no doubt was viewed by Brahmins as dharmic given the new ideology of nonviolence, because euthanasia supports *dharma* (by allowing an exception to the general rule of *dharma* in special circumstances). By this logic of the exception, it is likely that euthanasia was reconciled with the principle of *ahiṁsā*. (In a similar kind of argument, some Brahmins argued that ritual sacrifice was also a legitimate exception to *ahiṁsā*.)

Besides the principle of *ahiṁsā,* which helps to define the limits of the phenomenon of euthanasia circuitously through the legal idea of exception, another important restraint imposed on *mors voluntaria religiosa* is the idea of decision or resolve (*saṁkalpa*). The idea of decision or resolve is first given religious significance in the context of Vedic ritual. The declaration of intent to perform a sacrifice is formalized (*saṁkalpa*). So important is this pronouncement of intent that the ensuing action and even goal is but the automatic sequel of the resolve (with the qualification that the action be done properly). The resolve or will, therefore, generates a power and this willpower, so to speak, can define destiny. Over time, the concept of *saṁkalpa* extends beyond the sacrificial context to other types of religious practises, *mors voluntaria religiosa* notwithstanding.

According to Mīmāṁsā, the idea of command (*vidhi*) is related to *apūrva* or capability that always comes into existence as a result of action. If we understand public declaration of intent (*saṁkalpa*) as analogous to a command (*vidhi*) in that it is also viewed as a source of law (see *ātmatuṣṭi* below), then because *saṁkalpa* always relates to action and every action has productive force (*bhāvanā*), this action:

> produces the capability (*yogyatā*) in the agent to hold as his own the fruit declared by law as of that action. This capability, which was absent before the action and has come into existence only as the result of that action, is known as '*Apūrva*' in Mīmāṁsā. This *apūrva* rests in the agent of the action even after the overt act has perished, and continues to exist till the fruit of the action is realized. . . . This *apūrva* rests in the agent, for the act also rests in him" (Deshpande 1971, 154): [One must act according to law not to obtain rewards but] "because my act will make me capable (*adhikṛta*) for *artha* i.e. what is conducive to good or welfare. Thus the ultimate sanction of law is '*Moral*'. The '*codanā*' determines the validity, while '*artha*' determines the value of Law (*dharma*). This is the nature of *apūrva* according to the *Mīmāṁsā*, which is the ultimate sanction of the rule of Dharma (*codanā punarāsambhaḥ*) (2.1.5). The rules of law exist because this *apūrva* exists. . . . Every right or claim has to come into being as a result of Duty fulfilled. . . . Hence it is, that Mīmāṁsā jurisprudence starts with the analysis of Duty and not of right.
>
> (Deshpande 1971, 155–56)

The five sources of law in descending authority are (1) *śruti* (revealed or declared law which is authoritative because "The word of law is potent enough to convey the intended meaning and does not depend on anything else for conveying it (*anapekṣatvāt*)" (Deshpande 1971, 154); (2) *smṛti* (law as formulated by the authors of the Dharmasūtras and Dharmaśāstras; (3) *sadācāra* (custom); and (4) *ātmatuṣṭi* which originates in the desire born of right intention (*saṁyaksaṁkalpaja*) of those who act within the limits of the above sources of law.

Now we are in a position to understand why to will death. To will death is so powerful that it can burn up bad *karma* and thereby expiate sin. It can produce good *karma* and thereby direct destiny, including a visit to heaven. And it can even dramatically influence the course of destiny by (1) eliminating all *karmas* that cause bondage thereby triggering salvation, or (2) appealing to the Supreme Deity's grace to recognize this supreme self-sacrifice. Given the promise of these effects, we understand the importance of the intention (*saṁkalpa*), which is so intimately related to the goal (*artha*) through the intervening idea of willpower. This idea of formal (and publicly announced) intention and the resultant will power helps to separate the phenomenon of *mors voluntaria religiosa* from suicide done usually in private out of passion, depression, and so forth.

While Brahmin jurists endorsed euthanasia for themselves as well as others in the society, they also continued to acknowledge, by the sheer weight of tradition, some practises of self-willed death performed by Kṣatriyas as legitimate for that caste. The epics and later inscriptions, for example, reveal customs related to older forms of heroic *mors voluntaria.* The great journey to death (*mahāprasthāna*) described in the *Mahāprasthānika Parva*[16] of the *Mahābhārata* involves a circumambulation through various kingdoms (representative of the earth) until death occurs. *Mahāprasthāna* was possibly prefigured in the Kṣatriya custom of withdrawing to the forest (which, we argued, was sacramentalized in the *puruṣamedha* and *sarvamedha* (rituals) as well as in the Jaina ideal of fasting to death (*sallekhanā*).

> Aparārka (p. 877) and Par. M. (I. part 2, p. 228) quote several verses from Ādipurāṇa about dying by fasting, by entering fire or deep water or by falling from a precipice, or by going on mahāprasthāna in the Himālayas or by abandoning life from the branch of the vaṭa tree at Prayāga, the verses declaring that not only does such a man not incur sin but he attains the worlds of bliss. In the Rāmāyaṇa (Araṇya chap. 9) Śarabhaṅga is said to have entered fire. We find that the Mṛcchakaṭika (I.4) speaks of king Śūdraka as having entered fire. In the Gupta Inscriptions No. 42, the great Emperor Kumāragupta is said to have entered the fire of dried cowdung cakes. . . . The Rājataraṅgiṇī (VI. 1411) refers to officers appointed by the king to superintend *prāyopaveśa* (resolving on death by fasting).
>
> (Kane 1974, 2:927)

The idea of self-willed death by a yogi or enlightened one (*jīvanmukta*), however, generated considerable debate among Brahmin thinkers. They often disagreed regarding legitimation of this form of *mors voluntaria religiosa.* This is curious because there are two obvious connections between self-willed death by an ascetic and religion: being beyond passion, and being able to will one's death. The idea that the enlightened one (*jīvanmukta*) is passionless builds on the logic that the *jīvanmukta* is indifferent to life and death, either because there is no reason to will death or there is no reason not to will death. Theoretically, one is totally indifferent to the body after enlightenment and indifferent to whether one lives or dies. Accordingly, the yogi may or may not will death. A structural opposition develops between the idea of suicide as done by an individual out of passion and the self-willed death by an enlightened one who is completely beyond passion. We may think that such a structural opposition creates firm boundaries to the phenomenon of self-willed death by the ascetic. This, however, was not the case, for there was also the alternative view that there could be no final enlightenment until there was elimination of the *karmas* that defined the physical existence of the body. The body, in other words, was a constant reminder that final enlightenment had not yet been achieved. A yogi, therefore, may choose to eliminate the body through self-willed death in order to attain enlightenment.

There may have been several reasons for Brahmanical reluctance to endorse self-willed death by a yogi. One, of course, was the Brahmanical penchant to live out the entire life span, as .advocated in the *Ṛg Veda*. Because a number of Brahmins may have become ascetics and were attracted to the idea of self-willed death, Brahmin thinkers may have been particularly reluctant to endorse this form of *mors voluntaria religiosa*. Unlike the case of euthanasia—where extreme human suffering may be involved or the individual was virtually at the end of the natural life span—the self-willed death of an ascetic may have appeared to others as robbing life at its prime. If Brahmins and others were attracted to asceticism in early or middle age, their self-willed death may have been perceived as a loss for society, not to mention the families involved. Then, too, perhaps the practise of self-willed death was abused in that it became an easy way to attain enlightenment and bypassed years of asceticism and meditation. This returns us to the idea that the intention (*saṁkalpa*) to die and the resulting will power are so powerful that they can destroy *karma*, in this case all the *karmas* that create bondage. If some Brahmins were accepting the idea of a quick and easy means to enlightenment, then we appreciate Brahmanical ambiguity regarding the practise of self-willed death by an ascetic and the underlying logic that could be exploited.

The *Mahābhārata* makes passing reference to the fast to death by one who has gone to the end of the Veda (presumably, one who is enlightened) and who is twice-born (*dvija:* a Brahmin, Kṣatriya or Vaiśya).

śarīramutsṛjettatra vidhipūravamanāsake|
adhruvaṁ jīvitaṁ jñātvā yo vai vedāntago dvijaḥ||

abhyarcya devatāstatra namaskṛtya munim̐stathā|
tataḥ siddho divaṁ gacched brahmalokaṁ sanātanam||

> A twice-born (*dvija*) gone to the end of the Veda, knowing that life is impermanent, may abandon the body thereby fasting to death according to prescription. After worshipping the gods and honouring the *munis*, the *siddha* may go to heaven, the eternal realm of *brahmā*.
>
> (*Anuśāsana parva* 25.63–64)

The *Bhagavad-Gītā* (17.6), however, disapproves of starving the body:

> *karsayantaḥ śarīrasthaṁ bhūtagrāmamacetasaḥ|*
> *māṁ caivāntaḥ śarīrasthaṁ tān viddhyāsuraniścayān||*
>
> Those who mindlessly starve the composite of elements which is situated in the body, know them to be of demonic resolve.

While the *Bhagavad-Gītā* does not address the issue of self-willed death directly, it does place great importance on one's thought at the time of death determining one's future state:

> *antakāle ca māmeva smaranmuktvā kalevaram||*
> *yaḥ prayāti sa madbhāvam yāti nāstyatra saṁśayaḥ||*
>
> (*Gītā* 8:5)
>
> And at the time of death, whoever leaves the body remembering Me alone, he attains my being. There is no doubt about this.
>
> *yaṁyaṁ vāpi smaranbhāvaṁ tyajatyante kalevaram|*
> *taṁtamevaiti kaunteya sadā tadbhāvabhāvitaḥ||*
>
> (*Gītā* 8:6)
>
> Or also what ever state of being he thinks of when he gives up the body at the end, that very state he obtains, O Kaunteya, always becoming that being.

The first verse suggests that mediation on God at the hour of death will lead to salvation. The second verse indicates that other thoughts will lead to rebirth, whether in lower heaven, on earth, or in hell. Full consciousness at the moment of death is extremely important. It is pivotal to one's destiny and may even hold the key to salvation. Because the *Gītā* takes a stand against premature renunciation of action and severe asceticism leading to self-willed death, it may reflect a Brahmanical agenda to substitute a *thought* for the *practise* of self-willed death. In other words, what one thinks at the moment of death, one becomes or attains.

This thought, which accomplishes what is desired (much as *saṁkalpa* does) becomes an attractive solution to maintain the natural life span. Furthermore, a thought is much easier than death, and such substitution helps the Brahmins to compete with the ideology of self-willed death with its promise of attaining the ultimate goal. In this respect, it may be one solution to the issues surrounding self-willed death, one also that is capable of great popularity, for it is both easy and universally available. (In the later devotional tradition (*bhakti*) these ideas are popularized. One desired not only to think of God at the moment of death, but also to be at a holy place and to die there. Heaven or salvation could be achieved by this moment's thought, especially at the right place.)

According to *Manu* (6.49), a mark of one who has attained liberation is that he is indifferent to everything: "Let him not desire to die, let him not desire to live; let him wait for [his appointed] time, as a servant [waits] for the payment of his wages" (Bühler 1967, 207). But *Manu* (6.31–32) says that the ascetic may die "fully determined and going straight on, in a north-easterly direction, subsisting on water and air, until his body sinks to rest. A Brāhmaṇa, having eliminated his body by one of those modes practised by the great sages, is exalted in the world of Brahman, free from sorrow and fear" (Buhler 1967, 204). In the same text (6.76–78), we read:

> Let him quit this dwelling, composed of the five elements, where the bones are the beams, which is held together by tendons (instead of cords), where the flesh and the blood are the mortar, which is thatched with the skin, which is foul-smelling, filled with urine and odure, infested by old age and sorrow, the seat of disease, harassed by pain, gloomy with passion, and perishable. He who leaves this body, [be it by necessity] as a tree [that is torn from] the river-bank, or [freely] like a bird [that] quits a tree, is freed from the misery [of this world, dreadful like] a shark
>
> (Bühler 1967, 212).

The statements of *Manu* appear on the surface to be contradictory. On the one hand, the liberated one (*jīvanmukta*) is to wait for his appointed time of death. On the other hand, he may will his death freely on one of the modes practised by the sages. It is possible to reconcile these two statements by suggesting that Manu, in general, does not want the *jīvanmukta* to terminate his life prematurely. In other words, self-willed death should ideally occur in old age when the natural time of death is approaching. *Manu* (6.31) does allow a forest hermit suffering from incurable disease and unable to perform the duties of his order to start on the Great Journey (*mahāprasthāna-gamana:* walking until death overcomes).

Patañjali (*Yoga Sūtras* 3.21) says that by control (*saṁyama*, inclusive of the last three limbs of yoga) over *karma* that is fast-in-fruition (*sopakrama*) and slow (*nirupakrama*) comes knowledge of death (*aparāntajñāna*). In other words, the yogi understands *karma* to be of two kinds. With reference to the past *karma* or *prārabdha*, which will come to fruition in this life, he can have power over it through *saṁyama*. One of his powers, (*vibhūti;*

siddhi) is the ability to know, and more importantly, to determine the time of death. Accordingly, one of the eight *siddhas* enumerated by Patañjali is *prākāmya* or the power of an irresistible will, which enables one to obtain anything simply by desiring it. Another power is *īśitva* (sovereignty) by which one can rule "over all things and enjoy unrivalled glory becoming like a god, and even create and destroy creatures, past, present, and future" (Walker 1968, 2:349). A yogi can will to live or to detach his subtle body from his physical body. Consequently, he can temporarily disappear or create the outward appearance of death and change bodies. The idea that a yogi can know/determine the time of death suggests that he also has the power to voluntarily transmigrate. These *siddhis,* however, are to be distinguished from those powers that will put an end to the slow (*nirupakrama*) *karmas,* which will come to fruition only in future lives. Patañjali does not address directly the question of the self-willed death of the enlightened one, yet his discussion of *saṁyama* and the *siddhis* provides scope for extending the discussion to the context of one who is enlightened. For, in the final life when no slow *karmas* remain, a *jīvanmukta* should be able to know/determine the time of death. He creates no new *karmas* and, as before, has power over the fast-moving (*sopakrama*) *karmas*. Consequently, he is able to determine the time of death. By knowing the time of death, he can determine death. And by determining death, he may make sure that the body is eliminated at the appropriate moment. This logic can be derived from Patañjali.

If Patañjali does not spell out the possibility of the self-willed death of the enlightened one, the *Jābālopaniṣad*, recognized as a late text by most scholars, does. In general, however, it seems that Brahmins were reluctant to endorse self-willed death for Brahmin ascetics or *jīvanmuktas* (unless, following Manu, it was done toward the very end of the natural life span). It may be concluded that acceptance of the natural life span or self-willed death virtually at the moment of natural death (as in the case of euthanasia) was generally endorsed by Brahmins for themselves.

Śaṁkara (788–838 C.E.), for example, argues that one must live out one's life to allow the *karmas* to come to fruition. He implies that the moment of natural death signals the moment when there are no more *karmas* that create bondage.

> We should understand that right knowledge is the cause which renders all actions impotent. But the action by which this body has been brought into existence will come as an end only when their effects will have been fully worked out; for, those actions have already commenced their effects. Thus wisdom can destroy only such actions as have not yet begun to produce their effects, whether they are actions done in this birth before the rise of knowledge and along with knowledge, or those done in the many previous births.
>
> (Śaṁkara's commentary on *Bhagavad Gītā* 4.37; Sastri 1972, 150)

The Brahmanical desire to live out the natural life span is most apparent in the theory of the four *āśramas*, which is gradually expounded in the Dharmaśāstras. The idea of four distinct stages of life is grafted onto the ancient Vedic idea of the long, good life. The ideal of a hundred years remains, presumably to allow time for the stages of studentship (*brahmacarya*), householdership (*gṛhastha*), retirement to the forest (*vānaprastha*) and wandering along (*saṁnyāsa*). This plan may be seen as the Hindu version of the middle path, for it seeks a final synthesis of Vedic and Upaniṣadic orientations. The old Vedic values of prosperity and progeny are incorporated into the stage of being a householder. The value of longevity is promoted in the concept of the full allotment of time needed to accomplish all goals. The prescriptions of the Āyurvedic or medical texts are to be followed to ensure a long, healthy life (mentally, as well as physically, through proper diet, exercise, and discipline). The ideal of *vānaprastha* is an acknowledgement of the ascetic's customary withdrawal to the forest and the Kṣatriya custom of withdrawal to provide for a peaceful succession. As such, *vānaprastha* may have served a similar purpose: to encourage disengagement as a way to ease the transfer of power in the family. Moreover, *mokṣa* (or heaven) is incorporated as a goal for the last two stages of life. Individuals are to cultivate a life-affirming attitude, albeit with a yogic discipline, introduced in the very first stage and pursued seriously in the last two stages to nurture disengagement and achieve enlightenment.

Despite Brahmanical reluctance to endorse self-willed death by a yogi, in later times figures such as Jñānadeva (1275–96 C.E.; a Marathi Brahmin) buried themselves alive on attaining liberation. Jñānadeva, according to tradition, voluntarily ended his life in his twenties along with his two brothers and sister. They felt "they had accomplished their mission in life" (Walker 1968, 2:505). Another interesting case is the tradition about the Kashmiri savant Abhinavagupta (10th–11th century) (recounted by R. C. Pandey 1963, 23–25). It is said that, by the time Abhinavagupta started to write his *Īśvara Pratyabhijña Vivṛti Vimarśīnī*, he had attained liberation (*jīvanmukta*). The last scene of his earthy existence, upon the completion of his life's work, involved walking with twelve hundred disciples into the Bhairava cave never to be seen again. Pandey visited this cave and discovered that one area was large enough to accommodate forty to fifty people. He concludes that it is plausible that that Abhinavagupta went into the cave with some followers to take *samādhi*, "a natural termination of the earthly life of a person like Abhinavagupta" (p. 25).

Before we look at the great popularization of *mors voluntaria religiosa* that develops and how this, in turn, creates serious questions regarding the practise of euthanasia, it is necessary to take note of some developments in Buddhism. They, too, contributed to this pan–Indian popularization.

In the *Kathāvatthu* i.2 there is recorded the story of Godhika who no longer has the concentration to meditate on account of a painful disease. When he thought of killing himself by the sword, Māra, who represents the antithesis of Buddha and symbolizes evil in the Pāli Canon, approaches Buddha and says:

> "Your disciple wants to die; he has resolved to die. Prevent him. How could one of your disciples die when he is not yet an *arhat?*" But, as it is explained in the *Abhidharmakośavyākhyā,* Godhika reached arhatship just after he began cutting his throat. It is said: "Those who take the sword are without regard for life; they achieve insight (*vipassanā*) and reach *nirvāṇa.*" "Thus act the strong ones (*dhīra*); they desire not life; having removed thirst and the root of thirst (that is, ignorance), Godhika is at rest."
>
> (De La Vallée Poussin 1922, 26)

These examples are different from the earlier stories where enlightenment may have been prompted by a suicide attempt, but the enlightenment individual continued to live.

It is the last passage, in particular, that suggests that the practise of religious, self-willed death is being accepted into the Buddhist milieu. Curiously, Māra here seems to present the normative Buddhist position: that a monk or nun should not die before the natural span of life. The suicide of Godhika must have caused consternation to the monastic community. For the Buddhist teachings and example of Buddha's own life discouraged such solutions. That the question is projected onto the persona of Māra, and there is no reply from Buddha himself, suggests that the passage may be dated to a time when such Buddhist suicides were becoming more common. The official explanation, which appears in the later text *Abhidharmakośavyākhyā,* is that Godhika did indeed attain enlightenment at the moment he started to cut his throat. More importantly, such suicide is given official endorsement. Contrary to the earliest texts of the Canon, a new ideal is presented: the strong one (*dhīra*) who has no regard for life. The ability to take the sword[17] and to end one's life is precisely the state of being beyond attachment.

The Pāli work called *The Questions of King Milinda* poses a conundrum: a monk is not to commit suicide yet the Buddha said to destroy birth, old age, disease, and death. The wily monk Nāgasena argues that both statements are true. A monk is not to commit suicide because he must be a guide for others, and, at the same time, the Buddha instigated us to put an end to life to get beyond rebirth. Nāgasena's answer may be interpreted as endorsing self-willed death, if one has served as a guide for others.

Once religious, self-willed death is legitimated in Brahmanism and Buddhism in certain contexts, the practise gradually becomes popular. With Brahmanical support of the path of devotion (*bhakti-mārga*), the *tīrthas* or sacred places become one focus of the religious world view, and, more specifically, of *mors voluntaria religiosa.*

The concept of *tīrtha* is fully developed in the Hindu epics, *dharmaśāstras*, *purāṇas*, and *āgamas*. By now we find that tīrtha is associated with (1) any water, which is sacred by definition: rivers, lakes, falls, artificial tanks, and by extension any powerful feature of the landscape; (2) cross-roads and fords; (3) the place where the gods have crossed over to be present in this realm, that is, the temple; (4) the place to conquer or cross-over the daily problems of life, therefore the place to request boons from the deities to insure prosperity, posterity, and longevity; (5) the place to cross from one phase of life to another, that is, a place to perform the rites of passage (*saṁskāra*); (6) the place to cross from one life to the next, for example, the desire to die on the banks of the Gaṅgā or at any *tīrtha* or to perform the *śrāddha* ceremonies there; (7) the place to cross to another *loka*, that is, because of an excess of one's good merit (*puṇya*) a temporary, "vacation" in the paradise of heaven (svarga) or because of one's demerit (*pāpa*) a temporary "imprisonment" in hell (*naraka*); and (8) the place to cross to liberation (*mokṣa*).

(Young 1980, 63)

Since *tīrtha* is a place to cross over, it becomes a place for religious, self-willed death. The *smṛti* literature of the *Purāṇas* and the *Sthāla-purāṇas* eulogize the fame of holy places and *mors voluntaria religiosa* by praising how death there ensures heaven. Such religious propaganda served not only to popularize the pilgrimage places but also, in the final analysis, Brahmanism itself, which mounted a major ideological offensive after the 4th century C.E. on the heterodox religions by a spirit of universalism and easy accessibility to salvation. (These massive changes may be indicated by the use of the term *Hinduism* from this period on.)

yā gatiryogayuktasya saṁnyastasya manīṣiṇaḥ|
sā gatistyajataḥ prāṇān gaṅgāyamunasaṅgame||
akāmo vā sakāmo vā gaṅgāyaṁ yo vipadyate|
sa mṛto jāyate svarge narakaṁ ca na paśyati||

(*Kūrmapurāṇa*, I.37.16.39)

The goal which is obtained by the wise one—renounced, immersed in meditation—the same goal can be achieved by one who has abandoned life at the confluence of the [rivers] Gaṅgā and Yamunā. Whoever perishes in the Gaṅgā with desire or without desire conquers death in heaven and does not see hell.

jñānato 'jñānato vāpi kāmato 'kāmato 'pi vā|
gaṅgāyām ca sṛto martyaḥ svargaṃ mokṣam ca vindati||

(*Padmapurāṇa, sṛṣti* 60.65)

[Whether] knowingly or even unknowingly, intentionally or even unintentionally, a mortal, having gone [to death] in the Gaṅgā, obtains Heaven and *mokṣa*.

tasmātsarvaprayatnena tasmin kṣetre dvijottamāḥ|
dehatyāgo naraiḥ kāryaḥ samyaṅmokṣābhikāṅkṣibhiḥ||

(*Brahmapurāṇa* 177.25)

> O, best of the twice-born! Therefore the men who are desirous of *mokṣa* should sacrifice their bodies with every effort at this holy place.
>
> *śrīśaile santyajed dehaṁ brāhmaṇo dagdhakilbiṣaḥ|*
> *mucyate nātra sandeho hyavimukte yathā śubham||*
>
> (*Liṅgapurāṇa, pūrvārdha* 92.168–9)
>
> A Brahmin whose sins have been destroyed should abandon the body at Śrīśailam. Indeed, he is freed from the body here as at Avimukta (Benaras); there is no doubt about it.

It seems that the *tīrtha* called Prayāga, situated at the confluence of the great Yamunā and Gaṅgā rivers, was the ideal place for death by plunging into the sacred waters. Death here guaranteed immediate attainment of heaven. Similarly, the Gaṅgā and Vārāṇasī (Benaras) as the sacred river and holy city par excellence became places for such activity. The idea spread to other holy places, for the Sthāla-purāṇas advertised the fruit (*phala*) of pilgrimage (*tīrthayātrā*) and how easy heaven or easy *mokṣa* was available to all. Just how exaggerated the claims could be is demonstrated above: drowning at the *tīrtha*, whether voluntary or involuntary, produces the same result: heaven understood here as *mokṣa* itself. (According to *Matsyapurāṇa* 105.8–12, remembering Prayāga at the moment of death secures heaven. This is reminiscent of the *Gītā*.)

Competing with the *Purāṇas*, which popularize Hinduism, are the texts of Mahāyāna Buddhism.

In Mahāyāna Buddhism between the 2d and 6th centuries C.E., a new ideal type is popularized: the *bodhisattva* who vows not to have final enlightenment until all sentient creatures are saved. The *bodhisattva* dedicates his lives to helping others. The supreme form of gift is none other than self-sacrifice, even a gift of his body to feed a starving animal who is a sentient creature who must be helped and ultimately saved. Such accounts found in the Jātaka stories and Mahāyāna texts must have inspired Buddhist aspirants along the *bodhisattva* path to sacrifice themselves in imitation of the *bodhisattvas* described in the texts. In that such sacrifice is productive of merit and that such merit can be transferred to another, Mahāyāna ethics resemble the ethics of supererogation of the West.[18] Such Buddhist supererogation is carried to the extreme: beginners along the *bodhisattva* path sacrifice their lives to help another but also to accumulate merit for their own spiritual progress.

We have documented how the early Buddhist perspective is modified to incorporate the practise of religious, self-willed death. The antecedents can be found in the Buddhist texts themselves, though the growing popularity of the practise throughout the society after the 6th century B.C.E. certainly played a role in the Buddhist reevaluation. It is still a difficult question, however, how common such religious deaths were in the Buddhist Order. The Chinese Buddhist monk I Tsing (682–727 C.E.) notices on his travels to India that Buddhists there abstain from suicide and self-torture, unlike the Chinese Buddhist monks.[19]

It is not surprising that Jainism (which was the first of the major Indian religions to advocate religious voluntary death) extends this practise to the laity. In the *Uttarādhyayana*, the *Upāsaka-daśaḥ*, and the *Sāgaradharmamṛta* there is appeal to the laity to enter the Order, at least in the last stage of life.[20] The *Uttarādhyayana* (V.3) puts the matter succinctly: "Death against one's will is that of ignorant men, and it happens (to the same individual) many times. Death with one's will is that of wise men, and at best it happens but once" (Jacobi 1895, 20). Over time, *sallekhanā* is extended to the laity, without the intermediary stage of mendicancy. Four different contexts for the fast to death are enumerated in the Jaina law books: (1) unavoidable calamity (*upasarga*), which includes captivity by an enemy [and no doubt derives from the context of heroic *mors voluntaria*]; (2) great famine (*durbhikṣā*), (3) old age (*jarā*), especially when problems of disease, weakness, and senility start; and (4) severe illness (*niḥpratīkārārujā*). Once again, we find close association between religious, self-willed death and old age and severe disease, which brings us to the context of euthanasia.

In the Jaina context of euthanasia, *sallekhanā* is carefully regulated. One should obtain forgiveness and give forgiveness. One is to make a formal vow (*mahāvratamaraṇa*) after discussing all sins with the preceptor. Once the vow is taken, the attention is to be focused on scripture. Meditation on the real nature of the self is to be done while one abstains gradually from food and water. At the very end, just before the soul departs from the body, the *mantra namokar* is to be repeated. The necessary involvement of a *guru* and the making of a formal vow (analogous to *saṁkalpa*) by the lay person who is extremely ill is a change from ancient times when a Jaina mendicant could start the fast on his/her own. The practise is now virtually a ritual under control of the Order.

The popularity of the practise of Jaina *sallekhanā* is attested by numerous inscriptions, which became common after the 7th century C.E. (see Tukol 1976, 18–63). The epitaph on a stone slab, in short, serves as a memorial. (These Jaina memorial stones raise the question of the connection of the Jaina fast to death and the descriptions of heroic death and the hero and *satī* stones as well as the practise of warriors fasting to death in the Tamil Cankam texts.)

Because of the prestige and popularity of *sallekhanā* as the ideal Jaina death, a preferred option, it is fitting that the universal Jaina prayer is: "Cessation of sorrow, Cessation of karmas, *Death while in meditation, the attainment of enlightenment;* O holy Jina! friend of the entire universe, let these be mine, For I have taken refuge at your feet" (quoted by Jaini 1979, 226–7, italics added).

To conclude, between the 6th century B.C.E. and the 10th century C.E. there was increasing prohibition against suicide at the same time that there was popularization of religious, self-willed death. This development affected Hinduism, Buddhism, and Jainism.

Euthanasia was accepted by all religions. Brahmins, it seems, gave legitimation to euthanasia by viewing it as *mors voluntaria religiosa* and by defining certain limits to distinguish it from suicide. Brahmins also continued to acknowledge some forms of Kṣatriya *mors voluntaria*, especially where a connection to religion could be made. They were more reluctant to legitimize *mors voluntaria religiosa* by enlightened or virtually enlightened individuals, despite such religious dimensions as *saṁkalpa* or the state of being completely beyond passion. This reluctance, we argued, was because Brahmins themselves were often involved. Buddhists also were reluctant to endorse religious, self-willed death, but they, too, gave the practise textual legitimation. While the practise was rare in India, it became more common in Chinese Buddhism.

Eventually, Brahmanism (as it underwent transformation to Hinduism through its involvement in yoga and *bhakti*), Buddhism (especially through its transformation to Mahāyāna), and Jainism all compete with each other by stressing their universalism and by offering easy means to heaven or enlightenment. In this context, *mors voluntaria religiosa* becomes even more popular.

In the next section we shall see that as religious popularity grew, it was more difficult to maintain the distinctions between *mors voluntaria religiosa* (including euthanasia) and suicide. This resulted in reevaluation of euthanasia.

V. Criticisms of Religious, Self-Willed Death From the 10th Century C.E.

Religious propaganda regarding self-willed death was so blatant that the numbers of deaths instigated by such hyperbole may have increased considerably. Some lawgivers began to rethink the category by the 10th century C.E., as Hinduism emerged triumphant over Buddhism and Jainism. The Hindu lawgiver, Gautama had already opined "that no mourning need be observed for those who willfully meet death by fasting, or by cutting themselves off with a weapon, or by fire or poison or water or by hanging or by falling from a precipice" (Kane 1974, 2: 926). Since no *śrāddha* ceremonies or mourning was to be done for someone who committed suicide proper, we may assume that Gautama classified the above ways of death, which may also be means of *mors voluntaria religiosa*, as suicide.

While there was an occasional attempt to bar religious, voluntary death on the basis of *śruti*, it was only in texts describing the Kalivarjyas (dated by Kane from the 10th century C.E.) that we find systematic prohibition of the practise. The Kalivarjyas are actions once authorized in *śruti* or *smṛti*, which are discarded by the consensus of the good people in the Kali Age in order to guard people from the loss of *dharma*. In essence, they become a means to instigate reform. Significantly, *mahāprasthāna*, or going on the Great Journey by an ascetic suffering from an incurable disease, and the religious, voluntary death of very old people by falling into a fire or from a precipice (Kane 1974, 3: 939, 958–9) are now prohibited. The *Śuddhitattva* holds the view that religious death is allowed in the Kaliyuga only to *śūdras*. Others, for example, Nīlakaṇṭha, in his commentary on the *Mahābhārata*, argues that *Vanaparva* 85.83 refers to natural death at Prayāga, not self-willed death. The *Tīrthaprākaśa* forbids only Brahmins from performing religious death there. So strong is the debate over religious, voluntary death that those who do not forbid such death nonetheless place increasing restrictions on the practise. Kane (1974, 4: 609) notes that the *Tristhalīsetu* forbids the act by one who must support his old parents or young wife and children or by a woman who is pregnant, has young children, or has not received the permission of her husband.

The Kalivarjya prohibitions and the underlying debate point to a situation of abuse. This leads us to the question: was euthanasia prohibited simply because of its association with *mors voluntaria religiosa* or was it, too, subject to abuse? On account of the limited number of textual references, it is difficult to determine the answer. There are certainly some latent dangers in the practise of euthanasia. While euthanasia was always defined as an option and an individual had the moral responsibility to make sure that it was a legitimate case and not a situation of suicide or murder, for which he/she would go to hell, there may well have been pressures to will death. Take, for example, the religious idea of withdrawing to the forest (*vānaprastha*). As we have seen, such withdrawal was ostensibly to allow a man and perhaps his wife to begin the quest for liberation proper after their royal or family duties were finished. But they may also have faced pressures from the family to leave home and delegate their authority and financial resources to the younger generation. Such social pressure with its political and economic dimension may have led to a sense of abandonment, rejection, and pessimism on the part of the elderly. This, in turn, may have led to walking into fire or jumping from a cliff, more as a form of suicide than an act to attain the supreme goal. It is possible, then, that euthanasia was abused.

Despite the fact that euthanasia was the first form of self-willed death that Brahmins accepted, it is noteworthy that when euthanasia became a problem for society, a number of thinkers spoke out strongly against it and tried to formalize their protest as the Kalivarjya prohibitions. Of course, if *mors voluntaria religiosa* in general had become a serious problem for society, euthanasia, too, would come under scrutiny, since it belonged to this category of self-willed death. Probably abuse of both euthanasia proper and *mors voluntaria religiosa* accounts for the prohibition of euthanasia at this time.

Alberuni observed (11th century C.E.) the Hindu custom of religious, voluntary death including euthanasia and noted that, despite a special law prohibiting Brahmins and Kṣatriyas from the practise, it was still done.

> Now as regards the right of the body of the living, the Hindus would not think of burning it save in the case of a widow who chooses to follow her husband, or in the case of those who are tired of their life, who are distressed over some incurable disease of their body, some irremovable bodily defect, or old age and infirmity. This, however, no man of distinction does, but only Vaiśyas and Śūdras, especially at those times which are prized as the most suitable for a man to acquire in them, for a future repetition of life, a better form and condition than that in which he happens to have been born and to live. Burning oneself is forbidden to Brahmans and Kshatriyas by a special law. Therefore these, if they want to kill themselves, do so at the time of an eclipse in some other manner, or they hire somebody to drown them in the Ganges, keeping them under water till they are dead.
>
> At the junction of the two rivers, Yamunā and Ganges, there is a great tree called Prayāga, a tree of the species called vaṭa . . . Here the Brahmans and Kshatriyas are in the habit of committing suicide by climing up the tree and throwing themselves into the Ganges.
>
> (Sachau 1971, 170–171)

Despite the extended debate and the Kalivarjya prohibitions, the custom of dying at a *tīrtha* had such textual support in the *smṛtis* and was so supported by popular imagination that it proved difficult to eliminate. With the vociferous critiques of the Christian missionaries, however, the debate, reopened. Abbé J. A. Dubois, writing at the end of the 19th century, offered his caustic comment: "There are still fanatics to be found who solemnly bind themselves to commit suicide, under the conviction that by the performance of the mad act they will ensure for themselves the immediate enjoyment of supreme blessedness" (Dubois 1959, 521).

There is one other aspect of religious, voluntary death that contributed to the modern legal definition of suicide. That is the debate (also internal to Hinduism though intensified by missionary attacks) over the practise of *satī*.

The word *satī* literally means a "good woman" but conventionally refers to the act of *satī,* self-immolation of a woman on the funeral pyre of her husband or a woman who performs the act. We have already suggested that *satī* may be traced to a form of *mors voluntaria heroica* in the warrior circles in the Gangetic plain. Our reconstruction suggested that the women associated with warriors willed their death to avoid rape, capture, or death, especially when their husbands were captured or killed in battle. Gradually, the practise extended beyond Kṣatriya circles. By the time of the *Mitākṣarā* (14th century C.E. or later), *satī* is promoted as the ideal for all women. The medieval writers usually say such an act is dharmic because a woman is always "to follow her husband." Thus, *satī* is the act of a woman joining the cremation of her husband. Moreover her action is considered religious, not suicidal, nor motivated by a desire to escape the plight of the inauspicious widow for a number of reasons. The result of her action is said to secure heaven immediately for herself and her husband. The orientation of a *satī* may be termed *patiyoga*, discipline for and union with (yoga) the husband/god (*pati*) (Hejib and Young, n.d.). For these reasons, then, it may be argued that *satī* belongs to the category of religious, self-willed death. By the medieval period, it was considered a "good death," even the ideal death, for a Hindu woman. Like the epitaphs of the Jaina nuns who performed *sallekhanā*, memorial stones eulogizing the *satī* and her greatness were erected.

There were some, however, who opposed the practise of *satī*. Aspects of the debate over *satī* emerge in Vijñāneśvara's commentary called the *Mitākṣarā*, on the *Yājñavalkya Smṛti*. Vijñāneśvara himself supports *satī* and rebuts carefully those who do not. His discussion enables us to reconstruct what where common objections to *satī*. One objection raised is that the rule of *satī* does not apply to Brahmin widows. (Significantly, prohibition of *satī* is not included in the Kalivarjya rules. The above objection, however, sounds as though it belongs to those debates.) Another objection mentioned is that suicide is prohibited for both women and men because it involves "inordinate love of enjoying heaven" which transgresses "a prohibitory rule of law (which forbids suicide)" (Vidyārṇava 1974, 168). Finally, the objection is raised that one who wishes *mokṣa* should not die before the end of natural life, for the sake of attaining heaven, which is a temporary pleasure. In these objections we find a concern to ensure the natural life span, which we now recognize as a longstanding Brahmin position. One way to support the natural life span was to shift interest away from heaven by viewing heaven as a lower realm and transient pleasure, an idea conveniently found in the early concept of heaven (*svarga*). Once heaven is devalued in the scheme of things, then *satī* and other forms of *mors voluntaria religiosa*—which made heaven the automatic result of self-willed death—lost status as salvific acts. Such an attempt to replace the *bhakti* ideal of supreme heaven by the notion of *svarga*, however, was doomed to failure. In short, it was difficult to argue against the idea of religious self-willed death. The overlap of the phenomena of *satī*, *mors voluntaria religiosa*, and suicide remained.

In the forthcoming book: *Sati: Historical and Phenomenological Essays* (Sharma *et al.* n.d.), Arvind Sharma traces vociferous foreign criticisms of the act from the time of the early Greeks in India to the Muslims, Christian missionaries, and the British Raj. Because of the sensationalism of eyewitness accounts, Christian religious propaganda against "heathen practises," and even the Raj's justification of British rule on the basis of the need to foster morality in the population, Hindu leaders such as Raja Rammohun Roy take up the cause of reform. All this leads to Regulation XVII of 1829, which declared the burning or burying alive of widows to be culpable homicide.

With religious propaganda, on the one hand, and critiques of Hindu religious, self-willed death, on the other hand, the question remains whether voluntary death in Buddhism and Jainism was also subject to such debate. Śāntideva (about 700 C.E.), a Buddhist, had already questioned in his *Śikṣāsamuccaya* whether the sacrifice of one's body is really useful to one's fellow creatures:

> In what measure is a disciple—a beginner—to imitate the heroic deeds of the *bodhisattvas* of old? The disciple is ready, willing and resolved even to commit sin and to burn in hell for the sake of another, not to mention sacrificing his limbs and body; but he must avoid any mistake in the realization of his resolve. The question is whether in such and such a case sacrifice or self-denial is really useful to our fellow creatures; whether there is not some other means of procuring universal welfare. To sum up, the sacrifice of one's body is not in accordance with a wise estimate of the spiritual needs of a beginner.
>
> (De La Vallée Poussin 1922, 26)

Since Buddhism by the 11th century was in rapid decline and would soon disappear from the Indian subcontinent, the question of religious, voluntary death for Buddhists in India became a non-issue. It is interesting, however, that the Jainas continue to defend the custom of *sallekhanā*.

> In every case, Jaina teachers are careful to stress the need for "pure means" in undertaking a "controlled" death. They object strenuously, for example, to the sort of practice described in certain Hindu scriptures wherein yogins of a young age and good health are voluntarily entombed while in meditation, hoping to please their gods and attain endless bliss by this "self-offering." Jumping from holy peaks or disappearing into the sea while in deep trance are similarly decried. Though Jainas are willing to ascribe good (spiritual) motives to individuals who commit such acts, they nevertheless consider these forms of suicide to be absolutely improper and to lead one only to rebirth in hell. Jaina tradition is adamant on this point.
>
> (Jaini 1979, 228).

In other words, Jainas join in the critique of Hindu, self-willed death but justify their own version, which is described as carefully regulated. In fact, Justice Tukol, who is one of the first to challenge the modern Indian legal definition of suicide (see Introduction), is a Jaina. In the preface to his book *Sallekhanā Is Not Suicide* (1976, Foreword p. 3), there is an account of the fast to death in 1976 by the mother of Shri Chimanlal Chakubhai Shah, a leading solicitor of Bombay:

> She was suffering from jaundice. Medicines did not show good results. Doctors apprehended cancer of liver. She understood everything. She left medicines. She avoided solid food. After that she did not take even liquid food. She did not take in glucose through veins. Doctors advised her to get admitted to the hospital. But she requested her relatives to allow her to shun her body peacefully. She had no attachment to her body. She had no desire to prolong her life. Gradually her body waned but her mind was firm and peaceful. She took the vow of Sallekhana (=Santhāro) from Shri Kantirushiji, a Jain monk. She heard religious songs and cattāri maṅgala. On hearing the fourth maṅgala she passed away peacefully. It was 17th April 1976.

With the longstanding Jaina promotion of *sallekhanā* and its close association with old age and disease, it is not surprising that it is rediscovered in the modern world to deal with cases of terminal illness when treatment becomes ineffective. It is likely that future discussions may be spurred by the Jainas, for whom the fast to death is still an ideal. For they may argue, on the basis of text and history, that it is a good death and thus is relevant to the modern debate. Then again, Hindus, too, may be interested in the contemporary relevance of the fast to death. A Hindu equivalent of *sallekhanā* in the vernacular languages of North India is *prāyopaveśana* (abstaining from food and awaiting in a sitting posture the approach of death). Two modern Hindus who died in this manner are Savarkar, a Maharastrian freedom fighter who fasted to death in 1966 at the age of 83 and Vinoba Bhave who died by *prāyopaveśana* in 1982.

VI. Conclusion

The question arises: what can India today learn from the modern Western debate in the light of her own history on this topic and what can the West learn from traditional Indian views on euthanasia?

Perusal of the history of *mors voluntaria religiosa* including euthanasia in Hindu texts in the light of Buddhist and Jaina developments leads to appreciation of the importance of the interpretation of suicide in the Indian Penal Code written during the British Raj. The interpretation of the Indian legal definition of suicide as inclusive of *mors voluntaria religiosa* surely is a reflection of the longstanding debate internal to Hinduism, which was intensified by the missionaries' focus on the custom as inhumane and a fault of Hinduism itself. Although the definition of suicide was based on British law, it proved useful to help put an end to a variety of practises of self-willed death. While *mors voluntaria religiosa* was always viewed as an option based on the choice of the individual, there were certainly religious pressures for choosing this option, especially when it became a sign of, or a way to, enlightenment or heaven. There were also social pressures to instigate a person to choose *mors voluntaria religiosa,* such as pressure on the king or on elderly parents to leave the family as a way of transferring power to the next generation. The overlap in the methods of suicide and the methods of religious, self-willed death generated ambiguity, despite the strict legal definitions, making it often difficult for the individual and others to know what the real motivation was. This was especially true of the phenomenon of *satī.* It was eulogized, on the one hand, as the ideal death for a good woman and, on the other hand, may have appeared to the woman herself as preferable to the severe restrictions and social abuse of widowhood (therefore making *satī* into a type of suicide). Or, it may have appeared to the relatives as a way to eliminate a dependent and potentially disruptive female from their midst and take her financial resources (therefore making *satī* into a type of homocide).

The Brahmanical jurists and thinkers tried to eliminate such situations of ambiguity, but they obviously could not control all the extenuating circumstances. That they may have participated in the promotion of the religion by eulogizing self-willed death as an easy way to attain liberation or heaven means that they were sometimes willing to overcome their own misgivings if such propaganda were advantageous. Ensuring the loyalty of the Kṣatriyas, enhancing their clientele through promoting devotion (*bhakti*) as a universal religion and way to easy salvation, and safeguarding patriarchal control over women as in the case of *satī* were cases in point.

In sum, although there were attempts to prevent abuse, abuse did occur. Accordingly, euthanasia became a social issue and topic for debate. Euthanasia in the context of debilitating old age and severe disease—while originally endorsed by the jurists as an exception to the general rule to await the natural end of life (even for Brahmins, which suggests they felt keenly the merits of the case)—was swept up into the general debate over *mors voluntaria religiosa.* Perhaps because householder Brahmins were involved, euthanasia became one of the first forms of religious, self-willed death to be prohibited. One lesson to be learned from this study of euthanasia in the ancient Hindu context is that it is extremely difficult to limit self-willed death to certain contexts and to prevent abuse even when there is a strong religious disposition to live out the natural life span. A more general lesson to be learned from this discussion is that there is need to be constantly on guard to prevent abuse of euthanasia; we should not forget that today's large classes of the elderly and of individuals seeking permanent relief from AIDS, are potential victims of abuse in the West, as well.[21]

The issue of euthanasia in India is now being reopened since problems raised by advanced medical technology, which sparked the Western re-evaluation of euthanasia, are becoming an ethical agenda in India as well. While Jaina spokesmen have argued on behalf of the contemporary relevance of *sallekhanā* as a good death, the issue is sufficiently complex to necessitate analysis of all the factors involved. It may be argued that the paradigm of self-willed death has modern relevance or it may be argued that, because of past history, Indian law should maintain its definition of suicide as inclusive of *mors voluntaria religiosa*, including self-willed death in cases of debilitating old age and terminal illness.

The first approach does not debate the delicate question of whether any form of hastening death is morally justified, but builds on the classical Indian acceptance of self-willed death in cases of debilitating old age and severe illness in the light of modern discussions. Although the traditional Indian perspective had severe illness as one of the permissible situations for self-willed death, the overlap of this special context and other forms of religious, voluntary death tended to make the boundaries poorly defined. It may be argued, as Hindus have done, that, when self-willed death is accepted today on the basis of precedent in the Indian context, there should be an attempt to define strict boundaries. To maximize the respect for and support of life, death should be limited legally to cases of terminal illness. Furthermore, to ensure that the situation is veritably one of terminal illness, the medical profession must be involved. In other words, precaution must be taken to ensure that the decision for self-willed death is not made independently by the individual, given any difficult situation, but that dire circumstances are medically pronounced.

The Jaina practise in the past involved the preceptor and, by extension, the Jaina Order in the decision making and implementation for the laity. Any modern support for self-willed death should mitigate against autonomy of practise but also provide criteria for universal permissibility and control. Accordingly, the Jaina view of the ideal death as *sallekhanā* before disease sets in (in order to ensure the individual's control and mastery over the time of death) and the Hindu ideal of *prāyopaveśana* need to be reevaluated so that life is not terminated prematurely.

It may be argued that fasting to death in cases of terminal illness should be recognized for all Indians who face this situation, not just Jainas. That Hindus, as well, practised fasting to death provides scope for such acceptance by the majority. While religious groups may be called upon to help provide palliative care, religious counselling, and support, the broader framework should be medical diagnosis.

Then, too, Hindus have voiced concern that reassessment of self-willed death must proceed cautiously to ensure that any appeal to religious precedent does not reopen the larger issue of other forms of religious, voluntary death. A careful hermeneutic by religious leaders based on the affirmation of a long life (which was so central to the Vedas, the Hindu scripture par excellence, and shared generally by the other Indian religions, as well) should be developed. It may be asserted that with support of long life at the forefront of national and religious consciousness, self-willed death in cases of terminal illness may be safely reintroduced. By limiting the means of self-willed death to fasting, the overlap with other forms of religious death—which, for Hindus, included jumping from a precipice, into a river, or fire, and so one—would be avoided and with them the ambiguous boundary with suicide proper, which also involved such means. The issue of fasting is currently an important question in Western legal thought. While there is general acceptance of the conscious withdrawal of food in cases of terminal illness as a way of hastening death, there are many in the medical profession who feel that this act should not be done in hospitals with the support of those in the medical profession, because it involves doctors in a basic conflict: to prolong life or to condone that death be hastened. For those who accept fasting as a way to hasten death, it is acknowledged that one can refuse food oneself and that such refusal may be stated in advance in a living will. If one compares fasting to death and withdrawal of treatment, then they are both similar in that they involve an omission, that is food or life support. They are different in that the former is a sustained act of willpower, which is why it is sometimes viewed as a positive act of killing the self. But since fasting to death involves primarily the self and not the doctor's active intervention aside from the diagnosis of terminal illness, it may be more acceptible medically and legally. The real problem is the comatose person who is incompetent to make a decision. The question is whether a court order is necessary to make it legally acceptable to omit food.

Furthermore, it may be argued that the above definition of self-willed death would allow a religious dimension of dying to be preserved in situations of terminal illness, albeit under careful medical and legal regulation. In the final analysis, a good death is related to a meaningful death. One way to maintain a meaningful death, at least in a religious society such as India, is to recognize that its meaning is central to the religious Weltanschauung and religious practises of a lifetime. Similarly, meaningful death may be related to a willingness to come to terms with impending death.

It may be contended that, to the degree that the individual prepares for natural death by recognizing its imminent approach, then he/she may lessen the fear of death by the power of decision and the exercise of human will. Taking active charge of, or at least responsibility for, the intervening time between knowledge of imminent death and death itself is a way to come to terms with senseless suffering by deliberately choosing to court meaningful suffering, which can be experienced as a positive act of dying. Participation of the will in the dying process may provide mental calm and ultimately peace itself. Furthermore, the religious perspective also allows the family to provide support and face the inevitability of death.

In short, it is possible to define self-willed death in such a way that it comes to terms with both modern humanistic and traditionally religious expectations and thereby becomes acceptable to the population at large. Even for the person who does not hold to religious views of death, the act of facing terminal illness with full human awareness and participation may be central to a good, peaceful death. Being human, which includes the exercise of the will to the very end, is not necessarily a denial of life or in religious terms a loss of hope or refusal to be moral or spiritual, but rather, it may be argued, the very fulfillment of human nature.

In the first approach outlined above, a phenomenological solution is proposed to the issue of self-willed death in modern India that focuses on society's obligation to foster life affirmation, takes into account the traditional religio-cultural framework, and opens the debate to a cross-cultural perspective. This phenomenological solution brings together the modern criterion of medical diagnosis of terminal illness and the traditional idea of fasting to death.

Because some individuals may find it too difficult to fast to death, it may be suggested that the decision to die be aided. Help may involve the withdrawal of food or withdrawal of treatment in hospitals. The question may now be raised: is there justification for euthanasia as compassionate murder when a doctor administers poison to a terminally ill patient, given the traditional Indian views of euthanasia as self-willed death? It may be argued that it is possible to extend the traditional Indian concept of self-willed death to the modern definition of euthanasia as compassionate murder by suggesting that the traditional Indian public declaration of intention (*saṁkalpa*) is analogous to the modern notion of the patient's consent. Just as in the past, help, such as administering poison, was sometimes allowed once a formal intent was publically declared, so by today's modern definition of euthanasia the doctor helps the patient, once the patient's consent has been given in cases of terminal illness, by administering an overdose of drugs. While the traditional Indian view placed the emphasis on the will of the individual, the modern Western view places the emphasis on the doctor's action after the patient's consent has been given. Functionally, the two definitions allow for both the patient's will and the doctor's help to carry out the decision to die, even though the Indian phenomenon was closer to suicide given the emphasis on self-willed death, while the modern Western phenomenon is closer to murder given the emphasis on the doctor's active role in the death. Once again, it has been noted that both the Indian and the contemporary Western views sharply demarcated the phenomenon of euthanasia from the two extremes of suicide and murder, hence *mors voluntaria religiosa* and compassionate murder.

But compassionate murder is not yet legal in the West. Despite the attempt to build a bridge between the traditional Indian view of euthanasia as self-willed death with help and the modern view as the patient's consent with the doctor's help, there is still an important difference when doctors, who are to protect life, are assigned the task of actively hastening death through their intervention. For this reason alone, it may be preferable to keep the conceptual bridge between fasting to death and termination of treatment, rather than fasting and euthanasia.

Despite the ability of these arguments to address religious and humanistic expectations and thereby to bridge past and present, even East and West, there is another extremely serious issue. Pragmatically speaking, should the issue of self-willed death even be reopened at this point in Indian history? While such forms of religious, self-willed death as death at a *tīrtha* seem to be safely relegated to the past, some Hindus think that the legal definition of suicide is necessary to keep a constant check on these practises. The recent resurgence in 1987 of episodes of *satī*, the taking of cyannide by the Tamil guerrillas in Śrī Laṅkā to avoid capture, and the immediate sainthood of a Jaina who fasted to death are cases in point. Of the latter we read:

> Yesterday marked the 50th day since 82-year old Badri Prasad stopped eating and since the Jainist ascetic became known to his devotees as a "living god," named Tapasvi Sri Badri Prasadji Maharaj.
>
> Glistening with sweat, he is now too weak to speak to the hundreds of faithful who arrive daily to see him. "He is very happy," his son, 57-year-old Muni Ram Prasad, assures an outsider. "This is what he has always hoped for. He is becoming a saint."
>
> He is the first Jainist priest since 1948 to carry out the ancient death ritual. . .
>
> But Mr. Prasad's slow starvation has been labelled suicide in the Indian press—and likened to the Sept. 4 suttee of a young Hindu wife on her husband's funeral pyre that caused a national uproar. The Jainist practice is so rare, however, that baffled Hindus seem unwilling to do more than raise wary questions about legality. One prominent member of the faith, High Court Justice N. L. Jain, has gone on record as saying that no laws are being broken. "It is in accordance with our religion," he flatly

> informed the Indian Express. "There is no pain involved, as the body is in tune with God."
> (Bryan Johnson, *The Globe and Mail* (Toronto), Thursday, September 24, 1987, A8)

Indeed, it may prove difficult on account of strong religious beliefs to revalorize the Jaina and Hindu understandings of self-willed death. It is striking in the case of Badri Prasad that some of his followers are themselves fasting until he dies. Furthermore, busloads of Jains have visited the living miracle, and a young acolyte priest has said "I want to die like that, also. . . . I, too, hope to become a saint someday" (*The Globe and Mail*, Thursday, September 24, 1987, A8). Thus, it may be impossible to ensure that it is only fasting to death or poison administered by a doctor in cases of official medical diagnosis of terminal illness that is practised once there is the patient's consent to die. In other words, by again offering a positive evaluation of fasting to death, people may once again look positively on other forms of religious, voluntary death as well, and the endorsement of one practise may lead inadvertently to the endorsement of others. The religious sentiments thus reinvoked may override the new definition, which is limited to medical diagnosis of terminal illness. Just at the moment of the completion of this study of self-willed death the following appeared *The Globe and Mail* (Toronto: Dec. 17, 1987, p. A10):

> The Indian Parliament passed a law yesterday imposing the death penalty for people who help carry out the ancient Hindu ritual of *suttee*—a widow's suicide on her husband's funeral pyre.
>
> The measure, prompted by the death in September of a young widow in western India, unanimously passed the Rajya Sabha (upper house). It had been approved by the more powerful Lok Sabha (lower house) on Tuesday.
>
> The legislation mirrors a law already in force in the western desert state of Rajasthan and imposes a maximum sentence of death for abetting a successful *suttee*.
>
> It also imposes prison sentences of as long as seven years for glorifying *suttee*, and empowers the Government to dismantle memorials and temples relating to it.
>
> A woman who tries to commit *suttee* could be sentenced to six months in jail under the bill.
>
> Many Indians were shocked by the death of a Rajasthani widow Roop Kanwar, 18, on her husband's flaming pyre Sept. 4 in Deorala village.
>
> The Government charged Roop Kanwar's brother-in-law, who lit the pyre, with murder and filed lesser charges against 22 others, including the dead woman's father.
>
> In a charge sheet filed in the Rajasthan state capital of Jaipur last month, the Government alleged that the woman was forced on to the pyre and pinned down with heavy firewood.

Given the potential abuse if *any* form of self-willed death is allowed, a second approach to self-willed death in cases of terminal illness in modern India has also been deemed worthy of consideration. It is aware that reintroducing self-willed death so soon after having eliminated century-old problems associated with *mors voluntaria religiosa* may cause regression (especially since we know from the history of religions that in times of social, political or economic stress, particularly when identity is threatened, there may be a regression to religious practises that formerly embraced the religious ideal, and there is an increase in suicide). And it realistically acknowledges that it may prove difficult to ensure medical diagnosis of terminal illness, especially when many do not have adequate access to medical treatment. It would maintain the legal definition of suicide as all-inclusive and a criminal act. But, should cases of self-willed death in a context of terminal illness come to the attention of the court, the law would be interpreted generously.

In sum, both the theoretical and the practical dimensions of the issue of self-willed death in a medical context must be addressed by contemporary Indian jurists and ethicists to advocate the best solution for this particular moment in history.

From a contemporary Western perspective, a study of the traditional Indian view of self-willed death is also worthy of reflection. On the one hand, it provides evidence that self-willed death may be integrated into a religious perspective and give meaning to death. On the other hand, those who advocate freedom to die would do well to remember that even self-willed death can be abused, given political, economic, social, and religious pressures.

If the freedom to die has no medical and legal limits, it may have potential to be exploited despite the good will involved; such is the danger with the Exit Literature. Unrestrained advocacy of the right to die or the right to an easy death as propounded, for example, by the Hemlock Society, should be reevaluated from the perspective of the Indian evidence. This demonstrates how important constraints are in order to avoid a devaluation of life.

Throughout this study we have attempted to think about the topic of self-willed death positively. And yet our historical reconstruction, in the final analysis, causes us to pause and ponder once more the extremely difficult questions involved, not as a moral *a priori* but as a reevaluation *a posteriori*. It may be argued that the contemporary Western debate, prompted by developments in medical technology, should consider the historical and cross-cultural data on this topic.

It must be remembered that the West has had for centuries, thanks to Judaism and Christianity, a presupposition that individuals are to live out their natural life span. The West is discussing euthanasia with this presupposition still operant in its psyche. This does not mean that the West should take this presupposition for granted. For humane reasons, a strict legal definition of withdrawal of treatment is now viewed as acceptable. But the West should be wary of the freedom to will death in any circumstance. The ancient Hindus, too, had the presupposition of a long life. After the Vedic age this began to erode and, at times, was abused on account of the growing popularity of religious, self-willed death and sociological factors that may have pressured the individual to will his/her own death.

It may be argued that Western societies today do not share the same religious perspective that contributed to such abuse (the attainment of heaven by death at a holy place, and so on). It may also be contended that there may be equally serious situations in the future—from population explosion to the difficulty of caring for a large population of the elderly, from individuals suffering from AIDS to eugenics—that could easily stimulate abuse if societies fail to support the natural life span. Pessimism may be engendered in the modern age by other factors, such as living in the face of a possible nuclear holocaust or even deep questions on the meaning of human life when death is seen as the absolute end. Any perspective that contributes to the possibility of pessimism at the core of the Weltanschauung must be reevaluated. It may be far easier to erode life affirmation than to build it anew out of a pervasive pessimism. The danger lies in that, what starts out as a justification for an exception, such as euthanasia in special circumstances, may pave the way to a more general acceptance of self-willed death so that individuals take the matter into their own hands and bypass legal restrictions.

In conclusion, it may be said that there are good reasons for all cultures to be sensitive to the human dilemmas involved in the dying process. The issues involve not only the individual but also family and society. History, religion, medicine, and law must all inform today's reflection. It is hoped that the present study contributes to the ongoing discussion on a cross-cultural basis.[22]

Notes

1. This term was coined by Dr. Margaret Somerville, Director of the McGill Centre for Medicine, Ethics and Law, McGill University. I am grateful for a number of discussions with her that helped to refine my understanding of the current Western thinking on euthanasia.
2. *The American Heritage Dictionary*, 1969, 453.
3. See Paul Carrick's discussion in *Medical Ethics in Antiquity*, 1985, 127–8.

4. For details of the use of hemlock in ancient Greek society and the debate that ensued see Mair (1922) and Rose (1912). If euthanasia as the "good death" were associated with the drinking of hemlock and if controversy over the merits of euthanasia developed—as seems to be the case on account of the split over this issue among the various Greek schools—then it had probably become a problem for Greek society. This is no doubt because the practise had become common and not confined to situations of incurable disease and approaching death. The availability of hemlock may have encouraged suicide by individuals who faced any difficult problem or simply old age.

5. It may be argued that Jewish and Christian prohibitions against euthanasia should be viewed against a background of widespread suicide in Greek society (see Trowell 1973, 3–5). It is striking that the Hebrew Bible and the New Testament nowhere explicity condemn suicide, much less euthanasia, though the general Weltanschauung of both support the natural life span. Indeed, it was only after the Dispersion that suicide became more common among Jews and led to serious reflection on the issue (see Margoliouth 1922, 37). Given the lack of explicit prohibitions of suicide in the Bible, the contact of Jews with Greek society and consequently with the practise of euthanasia and suicide may have contributed to the emergence of the *issue* of suicide in Rabbinic writings and its strong condemnation.

   Just as Josephus condemned suicide as an act of self-destruction and running away from God, the early Church Fathers also addressed the issue. They, too, no doubt had to confront the Greek practise. While a few of the Early Fathers condoned suicide in certain situations, others prohibited it. St. Augustine and St. Thomas Aquinas spoke out against it. The three reasons provided by the latter in his *Summa* (II.ii.64,5) became the *locus classicus* of the Christian position: suicide is unnatural, an offence against the community, and a usurpation of God's power to give and take life. While martyrdom was understood as an exception, the general Christian view followed the position of Augustine and Aquinas in the later centuries. For subsequent theology acknowledged that God, the Creator, alone is the ordainer of life and death and that each one has a duty to preserve life. This view has been characterized as the principle of the "sanctity of life," which has its focus on God not life *per se*.

6. Insistence on due process of decision making is an attempt to protect the patient, especially the patient who is no longer able to make an informed decision but whose terminal illness and suffering make euthanasia desirable.

7. The one Western country that is practising euthanasia as compassionate death in situations of terminal illness such as AIDS, is the Netherlands. The government is currently moving toward legalizing it under strict conditions.

8. *Āyusmant*, a term of respect meaning "the long-lived one, sire," is used to address kings and monks. This, too, shows that long life is idealized, even though the life span may be short.

9. Examination of the royal consecration, the horse sacrifice, and the human sacrifice (see Keith 1925, 341ff.) reveals a number of Sagan's diagnostic features from gambling to harems, bardic poetry, riddles, ribald dialogue, sexual exhibitionism as well as suggestion of human sacrifice with reference to the *puruṣamedha*, the Puruṣasūkta (*Ṛg Veda* 10:90), and the rituals associated with Nārāyaṇa in the *Śatapatha Brāhmaṇa*.

10. Various arguments have been made regarding the origin of *mors voluntaria heroica* in India. Griffith (1968, 236) argued, for example, that *satī* is alluded to *Ṛg Veda* X.18.7–8 and *Atharva Veda* 18.3.1–3, but because the woman seems to lie down beside her dead husband only as a symbolic act and then arises, the practise must have belonged to the distant Aryan past, hence the symbolic remnant and the fact that the practise is called an ancient custom (*purāṇa*) in *Atharva Veda* 18.3.1. Griffith offers examples from "old northern poetry" to substantiate his claim. As noted in Note 11 below, the Homeric poems in ancient Greece also furnish several examples of self-willed death.
11. Both the Indian and Greek evidence (see Mair 1922, 27 for details of Greek texts) demonstrate a transition from support of the natural life span to acceptance of self-willed death. While there is some evidence in the Homeric poems of heroic, self-willed death out of shame, sorrow, and threat of rape (the examples of Epikaste, Antikleia, Erigone, Evadne, and the daughters of Skedasos), self-willed death was not explicitly linked to religious goals, for example, the attainment of heaven or liberation, as occurred in India. Rather, in the post-Homeric age, self-willed death was more an expression of the pessimism caused by the Peloponesian wars; with the discovery of hemlock, it became an easy means to commit suicide or to put an end to the suffering of extreme disease and old age. Despite the differences, however, it is striking that the historical examples provided by both ancient Greece and India show how easily and quickly the concept of self-willed death, when given societal legitimation, can erode a basic life-affirmation. The historical data from these two centres of civilization suggests that once legitimated, the practise becomes popular, and with popularity it is hard to limit the phenomenon conceptually and prevent overlap with suicide.
12. The word *ātmahanaḥ*, which appears in *Īśa* 3 has been generally understood by philosophers and modern translators as metaphorical in meaning: slayers of the True Self, or Soul, i.e., those who forget, neglect, or are ignorant of the Self. This metaphorical meaning is justified by recourse to *Bṛhadāraṇyaka* 4.4.11 which does not use the word *ātmahan* but says that people who do not have knowledge or are not awakened go to the worlds covered with blind darkness (*te lokāḥ andhena tamasā vṛtāḥ*). Since this very phrase *te lokāḥ andhena tamasā vṛtāḥ* is found in *Īśa* 3 as the destination of the *ātmahanaḥ*, the striking parallel must have given rise to the metaphorical interpretation of *ātmahanaḥ*. On the contrary, it can be plausibly argued though not convincingly established that *Īśa* 3 intends a literal meaning, "slayer of oneself," and therefore is a prohibition of suicide or self-willed death. This interpretation is feasible given the context of the previous two verses. One is to act renouncing greed and to live one hundred years. Such actions do not bind, since they are without desire and dedicated to God. Therefore one will be liberated, but those who kill themselves thinking it is action that binds will go to hell.

    In later times, there was some confusion regarding the interpretation of this verse. (Madhva and Bhavabhūti give a literal interpretation. Vedāntadeśika offers both metaphorical and literal interpretations. Śaṁkara, Kane, and Radhakrishnan give just the metaphorical meaning.) The question whether suicide is directly prohibited by any Vedic passage is explored in greater detail by Sharma and Young, 1987. For those who wanted a proof text for the prohibition of suicide, *Īśa* 3 provided one. More importantly, it refuted the theory that, since actions are binding and the body necessarily acts, one must eliminate the body for liberation. The message of the *Gītā*—act but without desire for the fruits of action—takes up the idea of the first three verses of *Īśa Upaniṣad;* the *Gītā,* however, stresses that the Self is never slain, 2.20.

13. See the stories of the nun, Sīhā, and the monks, Sappadāsa and Vakkali (Mrs. Rhys Davids 1909, 1:54; T. W. Rhys Davids 1913, 2:214).

14. Recognition of differences based on caste and stage of life led to the formulation of different codes of behavior for different groups, hence a "multiple ethic."

15. Dhṛtarāṣṭra is reminded that he had excessive indulgence for his proud son Duryodhana and paid court to those of wicked behaviour, which helped to instigate the great war. Because of such irresponsibility, he must experience the fruit of his own actions and should not give way to grief. Moreover, indulgence in grief never wins wealth nor what is desired, much less salvation. Neither scriptures nor the dead approve of such tears. One should not mourn dead warriors who have been slain in war, for youth, beauty, life, possessions, health, and companionship are impermanent. All must die in any case. Heroic death in battle ensures that the warrior will immediately gain fame and heaven. Others cannot attain heaven so speedily by sacrifices, gifts, asceticism, or knowledge. Those ignorant people who suffer or meet with destruction as the consequence of their own actions will not attain the supreme goal.

In *Mahābhārata* 15.49.9–38 we are told that Dhṛtarāṣṭra, along with his wife, Gāndhārī, and his sister-in-law, Kuntī, was performing austerities for six months during *vānaprastha,* the stage of life when they had retreated to the forest. Gāndhārī took only water and Kuntī had fasted for a month. One day they were sitting on the bank of the Gaṅgā in the forest when a fire broke out. Saṁjaya who was with them warned them of the advancing fire, but they were so weakened and thin by their austerities (*mandaprāṇaviceṣṭitaḥ*) that they decided not to escape arguing that "uniting with the fire we will attain the final state" (*vayamatrāgninā yuktā gamiṣyāmaḥ parāṁ gatim*) (*Āśramavāsikaparva* 15.45.23). Saṁjaya says despondently that this futile death by fire (*vṛthāgninā*) will be not willed/evil (*aniṣṭaḥ*). The reply is that, for we who have voluntarily renounced our home, this death is not not willed, i.e., it is willed or desired: (*naiṣa mṛtyuraniṣṭo no niḥsṛtānām gṛhātsvayam*) (26). Furthermore, dying through fire, water, or wind by a hermit is praised (27). They tell Saṁjaya that because he is not a hermit, he should escape the fire.

What is interesting about this account is that it is the antecedent to the concept of [self-]willed death (*iṣṭa-mṛtyu*) (which is the Sanskrit equivalent of *mors voluntaria heroica* or *religiosa*) and is viewed as legitimate for those who have become hermits or *vānaprasthins.* The source of legitimation is because "it is praised," in other words, there is an appeal to custom rather than scripture.

16. In the *Mahāprasthānika Parva,* the royal survivors of the great war decide to retire from the world to seek merit. Plans are made for an orderly succession of rule. Yudhiṣṭhira and his brothers offer oblations of water to the elders, perform the *srāddhas* of the deceased kin, feed the sages, bestow great gifts on the Brahmins and inform the citizens of their intention (*saṁkalpa*). Clad in the bark of trees, they perform the preliminary rituals, which are to bless them in the accomplishment of their goal, and begin their journey with their faces to the east, resolved to renounce the world with yogic discipline. They wander through

various kingdoms. They head south, southwest, west, and finally north. Their circumambulation of the earth completed, they behold the Himālayas and finally the grand peak of Mount Meru. The first to fall is the princess Yajñasenī, then Sahadeva, Nakula, followed by Arjuna, Bhīma, and finally Yudhiṣṭhira.

17. Perhaps the sword figures prominently here because Buddhism appealed to warriors. In Buddhism, the sword symbolizes the idea of cutting out desire and ignorance, thereby achieving wisdom.

18. For a Western theory of supererogation see David Heyd's *Supererogation: Its Status in Ethical Theory* (1982) and for a critique see Joel Feinberg's *Doing and Deserving: Essays in the Theory of Responsibility* (1970, 22).

19. It is thought that the Chinese practise is based on the account in the *Saddarma-puṇḍarīka* of Bhaiṣajyarāja, who set himself on fire, so dissatisfied was he with his previous worship.

20. *Sallekhanā*, for the laity, is legitimized in the *Upāsakadaśaḥ (Ten Lectures on the Religious Profession of a Layman)* wherein is described the death of Ānanda, a lay disciple of Mahāvīra. He undertakes *sallekhanā*, is reborn as a celestial being in the first heaven, and will be reborn in human form one last time for liberation. According to the *Sāgaradharmāmṛta* (i. 12), the lay discipline is to be completed by *sallekhanā*.

21. "It is questionable if today the young comatose patient is the prototype for the discussion of issues of death and dying. A more probable crucial issue is that of the elderly: a reservoir of relatively defenseless persons, perceived, through bigoted 'ageism,' as unproductive and pejoratively dependent. In them, modernization has created a population stratum that, in a state of nature or conditions of scare economic, 'ought' to be dead." (Gruman 1978, 267).

22. Our discussion has focused only on the dying person who is competent to make decisions and to will death. It has been rightly recognized that the truly difficult problems arise when one is unable to express wishes or make an informed decision. Without going into the details of this aspect of the contemporary debate, let it suffice to point to the report of the Law Reform Commission of Canada: "The law should recognize that the incapacity of a person to express his wishes is not sufficient a reason to oblige a physician to administer useless treatment for the purpose of prolonging his life; the law should recognize that in the case of an unconscious or incompetent patient, a physician incurs no criminal responsibility by terminating treatment which has become useless." (Law Reform Commission of Canada 1982, 66)

Bibliography

Amarakośa. ed. by A. A. Ramanathan. Madras: The Adyar Library and Research Centre, 1971.

Arunachalam, Thiru M. *The Sati Cult in Tamil Nadu*. Madras: Bulletin of the Institute of Traditional Cultures, 1978.

Basham, A. C. *The Wonder That Was India.* 3rd rev. ed., New York: Taplinger, 1968.

Bhattacharya, Batuknath. *The 'Kalivarjyas' or Prohibitions in the 'Kali' Age.* Calcutta: Calcutta University Press, 1943.

Blackburn, Stuart H. "Death and Deification: Folk Cults in Hinduism." In *History of Religions.* Chicago: The University of Chicago Press, Vol. 24, No. 3, 1985, pp. 255–274.

Bloomfield, Maurice. *Hymns of the Atharva-Veda.* In *Sacred Books of the East.* Vol. 42. F. Max Müller. Oxford: Clarendon Press, 1897.

Bühler, G., trans. *The Laws of Manu.* Delhi: Motilal Banarsidass, 1967. Reprint of 1886 edition.

Caillat, Colette. "Fasting Unto Death According to Āyaraṅga—Sutta and to Some Paiṇṇayas." In *Mahāvīra and His Teachings.* Ed. A. N. Upadhye et al. Bombay: Navajivan Press, 1977.

Callahan, Daniel, "The Sanctity of Life." In *Updating Life and Death.* Ed. Donald R. Cutler. Boston: Beacon Press, 1969.

Carrick, Paul. *Medical Ethics in Antiquity: Philosophical Perspectives on Abortion and Euthanasia.* Boston: D. Reidel, 1985.

Couture, André. "Note sur les diverse variétés de suicide en Inde." In *Les Suicides,* Coll. Cahiers de Researche Éthique II, Montreal, Sides, 1985, 129–147.

Crawford, S. Cromwell. *The Evolution of Hindu Ethical Ideals.* Calcutta: Firma K. L. Mukhopadhyay, 1974.

Dasgupta, Surama. *Development of Moral Philosophy in India.* Calcutta: Orient Longmans, 1961.

Davids, T. W. Rhys. Ed. *Pali-English Dictionary.* London: Luzac & Company, Ltd., 1966.

______, trans. *The Questions of King Milinda.* 2 vols. In *The Sacred Books of the East.* Vol. 35. Ed. F. Max Müller. Oxford: Clarendon Press, 1890.

______, trans. *Psalms of the Brethren.* In *Psalms of the Early Buddhists.* 2 vols. London: Oxford University Press, 1913.

Davids, Mrs. Rhys, trans. *Psalms of the Sisters.* In *Psalms of the Early Buddhists.* 2 vols. London: Oxford University Press, 1909.

"Death penalty approved for aiding Hindu suicide rite." In *The Globe and Mail* (Toronto). Dec. 17, 1987, p. A10.

Deshpande, Ganesh Tryambak. *Indological Papers.* Vol. 1. Nagpur (India): Vidarbha Samshodhan Mandal, 1971.

Dubois, Abbé J. A. *Hindu Manners, Customs and Ceremonies.* Trans. into English by Henry K. Beauchamp. 3d ed. Oxford: Clarendon Press, 1959.

Feinberg, Joel. *Doing and Deserving: Essays in the Theory of Responsibility.* Princeton: Princeton University Press, 1970.

Geldner, Karl Friedrich. *Der Rig-Veda.* In *The Harvard Oriental Series.* Vol. 33. Cambridge: Harvard University Press, 1951.

Griffith, Ralph T. H. trans. *The Hymns of the Atharvaveda.* Varanasi: Chowkhamba Sanskrit Series Office, 1968.

Gruman, Gerald J. "Death and Dying: Euthanasia and Sustaining Life". In *Encyclopedia of Bioethics.* Vol. 1. New York: Free Press, 1978, pp. 261–268.

Hejib, Alaka, and Katherine K. Young. "Sati, Widowhood and Yoga." In *Historical and Phenomenological Essays in Sati* by Arvind Sharma with Ajit Ray, Alaka Hejib and Katherine K. Young. To be published by Motilal Banarsidass.

Heesterman, J. C. "Non-violence and Sacrifice." In *Indological Taurinensia.* Vol. 12. Torino: Edizioni Jollygrafica, 1984, pp. 119–127.

Heyd, David. *Supererogation: Its Status in Ethical Theory.* Cambridge: Cambridge University Press, 1982.

Hindery, Roderick. *Comparative Ethics in Hindu and Buddhist Traditions.* Delhi: Motilal Banarsidass, 1978.

Holk, Frederick H. Ed. *Death and Eastern Thought: Understanding Death in Eastern Religions and Philosophies.* New York: Abingdon Press, 1974.

Hume, Robert Ernest, trans. *The Thirteen Principle Upanishads.* Reprint of 1931 Edition. Madras: Oxford University Press, 1968.

Jacobi, Hermann, trans. *Gaina Sūtras.* Part I. In *Sacred Books of the East.* Vol. 22. Ed. F. Max Müller. Oxford: Clarendon Press, 1884.

———, trans. *Gaina Sūtras.* Part II. In *Sacred Books of the East.* Vol. 45. Ed. F. Max Müller. Oxford: Clarendon Press, 1895.

Jaini, Padmanabh S. *The Jaina Path of Purification.* Berkeley: University of California Press, 1979.

Johnson, Bryan. "'Fast unto death' elevates Jainist to holy symbol." In *The Globe and Mail* (Toronto). Sept. 24, 1987, p. A8.

Kane, Pandurang Vaman. *History of Dharma-Śāstra (Ancient and Mediaeval Religious and Civil Law).* 6 vols. 2d Ed. Poona: Bhandarkar Oriental Institute, 1974.

Keith, Arthur Berriedale. "The Religion and Philosophy of the Veda and Upaniṣads." In *Harvard Oriental Series*, Vol. 32. Cambridge: Harvard University Press, 1925.

______. "Suicide (Hindu)." In *Encyclopaedia of Religion and Ethics*. Vol. 12. Ed. James Hastings. New York: Charles Scribner's Sons, 1922, pp. 33–35.

Larue, Gerald A. *Euthanasia and Religion: A Survey of the Attitudes of World Religions to the Right-To-Die*. Los Angeles: The Hemlock Society, 1985.

Law Reform Commission of Canada. Working Paper 28: *Euthanasia, Aiding Suicide and Cessation of Treatment*. Ottawa: Minister of Supply and Services Canada, 1982.

Mair, A. W. "Suicide (Greek and Roman)." In *Encyclopaedia of Religion and Ethics*. Vol. 12. Ed. James Hastings. New York: Charles Scribner's Sons, 1922, pp. 26–33.

Maquire, Daniel. "The Freedom to Die." In *New Theology No. 10: The Ethical and Theological Issues Raised by Recent Developments in the Life Sciences*. Ed. Martin E. Marty and Dean G. Peerman. New York: The Macmillan Co., 1973.

Margoliouth, G. "Suicide (Jewish)." In *Encyclopaedia of Religion and Ethics*. Vol. 12. Ed. James Hastings. New York: Charles Schriber's Sons, 1922, pp. 37–38.

Morris, William. Ed. *The American Heritage Dictionary of the English Language*. Boston: American Heritage Publishing Co., Inc., 1969.

Pandey, Kanti Chandra. *Abhinavagupta: An Historical and Philosophical Study*. Varanasi (India): Chowkhamba Sanskrit Series Office, 1963.

Poussin, L. De La Vallée. "Suicide (Buddhist)." In *Encyclopaedia of Religion and Ethics*. Vol. 12. Ed. James Hastings. New York: Charles Scribner's Sons, 1922, pp. 24–26.

Prasāda, Rāma, trans. *Patañjali's Yoga Sūtras: With the Commentary of Vyāsa and the Gloss of Vāchaspati Miśra*. In *The Sacred Books of the Hindus*. Vol. 4. Ed. B. D. Basu. Reprint of 1912 edition. New York: AMS Press, Inc., 1974.

Rose, H. J. "Euthanasia." In *Encyclopaedia of Religion and Ethics*. Vol. 5. Ed. James Hastings. New York: Charles Scribner's Sons, 1912.

Roy, Pratap Chandra, trans. *The Mahabharata: of Krishna-Dwaipayana Vyasa*. Volumes consulted 7, 8, 9, 10, Calcutta: Oriental Publishing Co. n.d.

Sachau, Edward C. *Alberuni's India.* Abridged Edition. Ed. Ainslie T. Embree. New York: W. W. Norton & Co. Inc., 1971.

Sagan, Eli. *At the Dawn of Tyranny: The Origins of Individualism, Political Oppression, and the State.* New York: Alfred A. Knopf, 1985.

Sarasvati, Svami Satya, and Satyakam Vidyalankar, trans. *Ṛgveda Saṁhitā.* Volumes consulted: 2, 3, 4. Delhi: Shiksha Bharati Press, 1977.

Śāstri, A. Mahādeva, trans. *The Bhagavad Gītā: with the commentary of Śrī Śankarāchārya.* 6th Ed. Madras: V. Ramaswamy Sastrulu & Sons, 1972.

Sharma, Arvind. "The Religious Justification of War in Hinduism." *ARC* (Religion and Violence II). Montreal: Religious Studies, McGill University, Vol. 13, No. 2 (Spring 1986), pp. 7–20.

Sharma, Arvind, and Ajit Ray, Alaka Hejib and Katherine K. Young. *Sati: Historical and Phenomenological Essays* To be published by Motilal Banarsidass.

Sharma, Arvind, and Katherine K. Young. "Īśa 3." Paper delivered to the American Oriental Society, 1987.

Sharma, I. C. *Ethical Philosophies of India.* Edited and revised by Stanley M. Daugert. Lincoln: Johnsen Publishing Company, 1965.

Sinha, Braj. "Religion and Violence–An Early Buddhist Perspective." In *ARC* (Religion and Violence II). Montreal: Religious Studies, McGill University, Vol. 13, No. 2 (Spring, 1986), pp. 20–29.

Thakur, Upendra. *The History of Suicide in India, An Introduction.* Delhi: Munshiram Manoharlal, 1963.

Thapar, Romila. "Death and the Hero." In *Mortality and Immortality: the anthropology and archaeology of death.* Eds. S. C. Humphreys and Helen King. London: Academic Press, 1981, pp. 293–315.

_____. *From Lineage to State.* Bombay: Oxford University Press, 1984.

Trowell, Hugh. *The Unfinished Debate of Euthanasia.* London: SCM Press, 1973.

Tukol, Justice T. K. *Sallekhanā Is Not Suicide.* In *L. D. Series.* Vol. 55. ed. Dalsukh Malvania and Nagin J. Shah. Ahmedabad: L. D. Institute of Indology, 1976.

Vidyārṇava, Śriśa Chandra, trans. *Yajnavalkya Smriti:* with the commentary of Vijnanaesvara called The Mitaksara. Book I: The Āchāra Adhyāya. In *The Sacred Books of the Hindus.* Vol. 21. Ed. B. D. Basu. Reprint of 1918 edition. New York: AMS Press, Inc., 1974.

Walker, Benjamin. *Hindu World: An Encyclopedic Survey of Hinduism.* 2 vols. London: George Allen & Unwin Ltd., 1968.

Wiltshire, Martin G. "The 'Suicide' Problem in the Pāli Canon." In the *Journal of the International Association of Buddhist Studies.* Vol. 6, No. 2, 1983.

Young, Katherine K. "Tīrtha and the Metaphor of Crossing Over." In *Studies in Religion/Sciences Religieuses.* Vol. 12, No. 1, 1983, pp. 61–68.

About the Authors

Harold G. Coward is Professor of Religious Studies and Director, The Calgary Institute for the Humanities, The University of Calgary. He received his Ph.D. from McMaster University and was a Research Fellow at Banaras Hindu University and Madras University in India. Publications include *Bhartṛhari* (1976), *Sphoṭa Theory* (1980), *Studies in Indian Thought* (1983), *Jung and Eastern Thought* (1985), *Pluralism: Challenge to World Religions* (1985), *Sacred Word and Sacred Text: Scripture in World Religions* (1988), and *The Philosophy of Grammar* (1988). In 1988 he gave "the T. R. V. Murti Memorial Lectures" at Banaras Hindu University.

Julius J. Lipner is Lecturer in the Comparative Study of Religion, Faculty of Divinity, Cambridge University and a Fellow of St. Edmund's College at Cambridge University. After his early university studies in India he obtained his Ph.D. in the History and Philosophy of Religion, King's College, London. He has lectured widely in England, India, Canada and the United States. Publications include *The Face of Truth: A Study of Meaning and Metaphysics in the Vedantic Theology of Ramanuja* (1986) and articles on Indology and Inter-religious Understanding. He is currently completing a book on the Bengali Brahmin, Brahmabandhab Upadhyay (1861–1907).

Katherine K. Young is Associate Professor in the Faculty of Religious Studies, at McGill University, Montreal, Quebec, Canada. She received her M.A. from the University of Chicago and Ph.D. from McGill University in the History of Religions with specialization in Hinduism. She has periodically studied and done research in India and has published in several main areas; religion in South India, women in Hinduism, and ethics. The McGill Studies in the History of Religions is appearing under her general editorship.

Index